Praise for MANAGING THE MOTHERLOAD

"*Managing the Motherload* will help anyone—not just mothers—learn simple and powerful ways to get the seemingly endless job of mothering and nurturing adequately done without losing their health, sense of humor, or sanity. As the mother of five, Bex knows exactly what she is talking about. And what she teaches, *works!*"

— **Christiane Northrup, M.D.**, *New York Times* best-selling author of *Women's Bodies, Women's Wisdom* and *Goddesses Never Age*

"*Managing the Motherload* is about navigating motherhood with vulnerability, grace, and self-forgiveness. It's a book about making room for ancestral healing. And this is a book in which you'll find your own ways to create a life that's reflective of your values. Rebekah's way of sharing is gold for us all."

— **Elena Brower**, best-selling author of *Practice You* and *Art of Attention*

"When I first became a mom, I felt like I was doing motherhood all wrong. In *Managing the Motherload*, Rebekah becomes the friend or sister I wish I had during those times to tell me, 'I've been there, and you're doing it all right.' Add the humor and transparency of Rebekah's personal stories to the real-world wisdom offered on every page, and you get a book I know you'll fall in love with."

— **Andrea Owen**, speaker, life coach, and author of
How to Stop Feeling Like Sh*t

"Inner peace doesn't mean everything around you has to be peaceful. Rebekah teaches you how to focus on what really matters while embracing the messy and magnificent journey of being a mom."

— **Jessica Ortner**, *New York Times* best-selling author of *The Tapping Solution for Weight Loss and Body Confidence*

"I honestly don't know how Rebekah does it. She runs a business, a farm, and a family of seven! I have one daughter and feel like she could run circles around me. If you want a peek into how to manage it all while keeping love at the forefront of everything you do, *Managing the Motherload* is for you. You will feel like you could do anything. Because you can!"

— **Erin Stutland**, author of *Mantras in Motion: Manifesting What You Want through Mindful Movement*

"How does a mother of five and meditation teacher handle it all? With humor, deep self-care, and authenticity. *Managing the Motherload* is not a parenting advice book; this is an inspirational guide for all mothers to love themselves through their struggles and become whole women in the process."

— **Alexandra Jamieson**, host of Her Rules Radio podcast and best-selling author of *Women, Food, and Desire*

"*Managing the Motherload* made me feel relaxed and capable. But here's what's different about this book and Rebekah's way than other resources for moms out there: this one reminded me that I don't need to be different than I already am to manage it all. She showed me how I could be exactly the kind of mother I'm meant to be with exactly what I already have within me— a gift that every mother on the planet deserves."

— **Kate Northrup**, best-selling author of *Do Less*

"With humor and humility, and with hard-won wisdom that only comes from lived experience, Rebekah reminds us that motherhood is an initiation; it's a spiritual path to embody love more fully with each next messy day and each next sacred breath."

— **Meggan Watterson**, author of *Mary Magdalene Revealed*

"During my pregnancy, I was fortunate enough to have Rebekah on my speed dial. She was my doula, and her guidance, support, and reassurance were priceless as I stepped into motherhood. Now, any mama-to-be or mama can have Rebekah as a resource with *Managing the Motherload*. This book is packed with practical tips that will help you navigate what is most likely the biggest, toughest, and most rewarding job of your life."

— **Robyn Youkilis**, wellness expert and best-selling author of *Go with Your Gut*

"Motherhood is complicated, messy, heartbreaking, and heart opening. Rebekah gets that, captures that, and shows you how to align yourself to the universal wisdom that this journey of life holds, while also handling the to-dos of everyday life. If you're seeking to be heard and understood both as a mom and as a woman, *Managing the Motherload* is your book."

— **Jennipher Walters**, co-founder of Fit Bottomed Girls and Fit Bottomed Girls podcast and co-author of *The Fit Bottomed Girls Anti-Diet*

"As a single father of two who was raised by a single mother, the raw honesty and realness of Rebekah's story is one I respect, honor, admire, and relate to. *Managing the Motherload* is not a book for just mothers—it is a book for all people!"

— **Quentin Vennie**, Vice President of the Yoga Alliance Foundation and author of *Strong in the Broken Places*

"As the creator of @nobullshitmotherhood, I feel I have found a soul sister in Rebekah, except she has four more kids than me (bless her). Rebekah demonstrates how to live an authentic life without losing your sense of humor or your sense of self. This is the parenting book I have been waiting for. This is the parenting book I wish I'd written. I hesitate even to call it a parenting book, as it's so much more. *Managing the Motherload* is a manual for living."

— **Jennifer Pastiloff**, author of *On Being Human: A Memoir of Waking Up, Living Real, and Listening Hard*

"Rebekah is a beacon of hope for moms who feel like they're lost at sea in this motherhood thing. Her courage, sincerity, and open communication shines a light on her own imperfections while recognizing that we're all just doing the best we can. *Managing the Motherload* reminds us that we're not alone, but instead, part of a powerful community of women. And by surrendering to the journey, we can each get a little closer to managing it all."

— **Nacia Walsh**, actress, parenting contributor, and mom of four

"If there was ever a woman that I trusted to guide me through managing motherhood, it's Rebekah Borucki. Through her authentic words, vulnerable sharing, and rooted, accessible guidance, I continuously feel less alone as a mother and human. Rebekah has a way of opening my eyes, ears, and heart to the truth of what it means to be a parent, by reminding me that through awareness and presence, the life I wish to lead as a mother is always possible."

— **Anna Gannon**, community and social media lead at Expectful, meditation teacher, and mother of two

"I'm not even a birth mother, and this book is full of useful and applicable wisdom for my life because it's rooted in love and lived experience. In an age of social media influencers, where people can award themselves with a platform with the touch of a button, it is beyond relieving to encounter 'real ones' who remind us that integrity and deep practice have not gone out of style. Rebekah Borucki is such a real one. Tell your friends."

— **Elizabeth DiAlto**, host of the Truth Telling podcast, creator of Wild Soul Movement, coach, stand-up comedian, and author of *Untame Yourself*

"In a time when motherhood brings so much pressure—to be the perfect mother, with the perfect children, and the perfect job, all while juggling life's myriad responsibilities—Rebekah shines a light on the many imperfections (and sometimes straight-up insanity) that come with being a parent. In *Managing the Motherload*, she shares her experience of motherhood from the intensely hard stuff to the overly joyful moments in a completely raw and honest way, all while keeping it real with her keen sense of humor. I think every mother will appreciate this book!"

— **Nicole Jardim**, certified women's health coach, creator of Fix Your Period, and co-author of *The Happy Balance*

"*Managing the Motherload* permits us to release what we think motherhood should look like and guides us to explore and call in our most expansive, yet accessible version of it. Rebekah lets us off the hook of expectation, helps us home in on our true knowing, and leaves generational trauma in the past, where it belongs. This gem of a book is a map towards holistic motherhood and a clear and bright family life."

— **Margaret Nichols**, founder of DIVINE FEMME and resident meditation consultant at The Motherhood Center of New York

"*Managing the Motherload* takes on the often harrowing aspects of motherhood with honesty and frankness, allowing mothers to give themselves the grace and peace they might not otherwise achieve. Her willingness to discuss her own struggles and successes, written in a convivial, relatable style, engages readers by guiding them on a journey of empathetic learning. It is clear that Rebekah has the utmost respect not only for her audience but mothers as a whole."

— **Cat Bowen**, lifestyle writer at Romper

"Rebekah wears her soul on her sleeve, sharing profound personal insights in a way that breaks down walls and allows the feelings we all have as mothers—helplessness, failure, pride, fear, and utter joy—to come rushing to the surface. The tools she offers up to excavate and process these moments are straightforward and vital. The 'village' is alive as ever within the pages of this very important, very human book."

— **Chondra Echert**, *New York Times* best-selling co-author of *The Armory Wars*, *Translucid*, and *Key of Z*, and the mother of one small dragon child

IT TAKES A VILLAGE

Managing the Motherload is a practice best approached with a tool kit of resources and a community of women to support you. There's no reason to go at it alone. I'm confident this book is going to be a terrific tool for you, and I'm thrilled that you're reading it right now, but this doesn't have to be where our journey together ends. I want to invite you to add to your tool kit with these free resources.

YOUR BOOK BONUSES ARE WAITING FOR YOU.

I have created exclusive free bonus gifts for my readers. All you have to do is register your book purchase at **BexLife.com/book**. There, you'll find details about how to access exclusive videos, workshops, and reader-only giveaways.

FIND ME ONLINE FOR DAILY MUSINGS ON MOTHERHOOD AND MORE.

Visit BexLife.com for more content to support your journey, including hundreds of videos on nutrition, exercise, meditation, and all other aspects of wellness. You'll also find links to join me on social media, where I share daily inspirational and motivational messages (and some truly transparent scenes from the motherhood trenches). My favorite places to hang out are on Instagram **@BexLife** and in my private group on Facebook (more on that next).

JOIN BLISSED IN ON FACEBOOK.

Looking for compassionate, nonjudgmental support from a like-minded village of women (and some phenomenal guy allies)? We're waiting for you in my free private Facebook group! Join my community of thousands of amazing souls for intimate, enlightening, and transformative conversations about motherhood, womanhood, personal and spiritual development, and so much more. Visit **BlissedInCommunity .com** to join.

SHOW YOUR LOVE FOR *MANAGING THE MOTHERLOAD*!

Meeting my readers on social media makes my heart jump for joy. Remember to share your selfies (and "shelfies") with the MTM community by using the official **#ManagingTheMother load** hashtag on Instagram. I can't wait to see your beautiful faces and reading spaces.

MANAGING
the
MOTHER
LOAD

Also by Rebekah Borucki

You Have 4 Minutes to Change Your Life

The above is available at your local bookstore,
or may be ordered by visiting:

Hay House USA: www.hayhouse.com®
Hay House Australia: www.hayhouse.com.au
Hay House UK: www.hayhouse.co.uk
Hay House India: www.hayhouse.co.in

MANAGING *the* MOTHER LOAD

A GUIDE TO CREATING MORE EASE, SPACE, *and* GRACE IN MOTHERHOOD

REBEKAH BORUCKI

HAY HOUSE, INC.
Carlsbad, California • New York City
London • Sydney • New Delhi

Published in the United States by: Hay House, Inc.: www.hayhouse.com®
Published in Australia by: Hay House Australia Pty. Ltd.: www.hayhouse.com.
au • *Published in the United Kingdom by:* Hay House UK, Ltd.: www.hayhouse
.co.uk • *Published in India by:* Hay House Publishers India: www.hayhouse.co.in

Cover design: Karla Baker
Interior design: Nick C. Welch
Interior illustrations: Danielle Pioli

Library of Congress Cataloging-in-Publication Data

Name: Borucki, Rebekah, author.
Title: Managing the motherload : a guide to creating more ease, space, and grace
in motherhood / Rebekah Borucki.
Description: 1st Edition. | Carlsbad : Hay House Inc., 2019.
Identifiers: LCCN 2019016777| ISBN 9781401956929 (paperback) | ISBN
   9781401956936 (ebook) | ISBN 9781401956943 (audiobook)
Subjects: LCSH: Motherhood. | Parenting. | Self-actualization (Psychology) |
   BISAC: FAMILY & RELATIONSHIPS / Parenting / Motherhood. | SELF-HELP /
   Stress Management. | SELF-HELP / Personal Growth / Success.
Classification: LCC HQ759 .B658 2019 | DDC 306.874/3--dc23 LC record
available at https://lccn.loc.gov/2019016777

Tradepaper ISBN: 978-1-4019-5692-9
e-book ISBN: 978-1-4019-5693-6
Audiobook ISBN: 978-1-4019-5694-3

10 9 8 7 6 5 4 3 2 1
1st edition, August 2019

Printed in the United States of America

For Mom, Dani, and Aunt Kathy

*"Go," she whispered. "Go. Show them you spell
your name W-O-M-A-N."*
— Maya Angelou

CONTENTS

INTRODUCTION

This isn't really a parenting book, and I'm not a parenting expert. I'm just a parent. If you're looking for the latest tips and tricks to get your toddler to bed without a level-10 tantrum or the secret to convincing your teenager to clean their room without a cash bribe, look elsewhere.

Many nights as my head hits the pillow, I look across the bed (over a sleeping preschooler with a tablet still in her hands) and say into my husband's exhausted eyes, "I don't know how long we can keep this up. I think they might be killing us."

I can't promise that when you're done with this book your children will listen to you, your house will look like it's been cleaned by an entourage of housekeeping fairies, or you won't still rely on the occasional bribe to get some peace and quiet. What I can promise you is that you'll have more focus, less stress, and more energy to manage it all.

I'm not here to give a lecture. I much prefer discussions. So, if you're a mom who just needs to sit down with a friend for a hot cup of tea and some helpful collaboration, conversation, and a moment to just breathe, I think the next 200-plus pages will be worth your super-precious time (and trust me, I do understand how super precious that time is).

Because though I would be willing to argue with anyone who dares to call me a parenting expert, the fact is that I am a parent of five children. And they haven't killed us—yet. That says something, right?

I get how hard it can be. I understand what it's like to hide in the laundry room, to cry in the shower, to wonder if it's possible to actually die from sleep deprivation (short answer: yes). But on the other side of all those short years and long days, I also count among my greatest blessings all those missed showers, the sweet smell of sweaty baby heads, the Cheerios under the couch cushions, and the dark nights when it's just me and a baby and the rest of the world is asleep.

The main reason I have resisted the title of parenting expert is that I'm really only the expert on parenting five children—Winona, Calvin, Jack, Sunny, and Annabel. And considering the number of tears, tantrums, and messes I find myself managing every day, I'm not even sure I'm that great of an expert. And those are just *my* messes. Add the chaos, drama, and comedic antics children bring to the mix, and it's a wonder that anything gets done around my house. But that's the funny thing—it does.

The important stuff always gets done. And maybe that's the one area in which I guess I do kind of know what I am doing. The big stuff is taken care of—despite all the tears and tantrums. And through it all, I have found gratitude for that messiness. The motherload hasn't just made me a mom; it's made me a better person. It has taught me how to manage stress, disappointment, success, and joy in ways that I don't know I would have been able to access otherwise. Though I am no expert on parenting, being a parent has forced me to become an expert in life (at least 15 percent of the time).

"Deep and simple is far more essential than shallow and complex."
— Fred Rogers

What I do hope you find by the end of this book is a way to navigate through all the big and small trials of motherhood and womanhood without losing yourself (or your sanity) in the process. The past several years have been the most turbulent of my life, complete with abundant joy and immeasurable grief. My husband and I welcomed our fifth baby into the world, and I saw many of my greatest career dreams come true. I have been able to build an extraordinary community of women around yoga, meditation, holistic health, and healing (and still get to be home with my children). And in the midst of all that celebration, I suffered a miscarriage, financial hardship, trouble in my marriage, and the loss of my father, mother, and stepfather over a short and devastating three-year period.

The stories, tools, and exercises that I'm offering in these pages will support you through almost anything life throws at you. My core belief is that profound healing can be found in the simplest of methods: stay in the moment, take one step at a time, and know that you have the power to change the course of your life and create your own happiness every day.

The Power of Surrender

I have five beautiful children who all shine in their own way. And I have loved every moment of seeing their unique personalities and talents emerge. When I was pregnant with my fourth baby, I was seeing a midwife who didn't order routine ultrasounds, which is a pretty normal practice for a healthy pregnancy. My husband and I were anxious to know the sex of our baby, so we decided to get one on our own. When I told my midwife, Louise, she said the truest thing that's ever been said to me about motherhood: "You can find out *what* you're going to get, but you can never know *who* you're going to get," she cautioned.

She was so right. Each one of my children couldn't be more different from their siblings, and my fourth baby, Sunny, wins the prize for delivering more unexpected surprises every day. Louise's message was not only wise, it was prophetic. It's been my greatest joy—and dutiful practice—to witness my children's growth rather than burdening them with my expectations for how they should or could be (and that's not always easy, I promise). Of course, there are times when I have to share a cautionary tale or advise them of what I think would be best, but I try to do it in alignment with the wisdom Louise shared with me. Perhaps one of the greatest gifts I have been given in parenting is the understanding that my children's journeys are not mine. They have each been blessed with their own rites of passage that are not mine to direct, and knowing that gives me at least a little bit of freedom from worry and control (only a little bit because I'm still a mother, after all). It offers me surrender.

And that just might be the biggest lesson I have gained from motherhood: the terrible, no fun, joyous act of surrender. I didn't get there easily; no one ever does. The whole point of surrender is that we are giving up the fight, which means we were busy fighting in the first place. And if you're anything like me, you don't let go of things without leaving a few claw marks. But surrender isn't just about waving the white flag, it's about understanding that everything we'd like to be in our control is not necessarily ours to manage or protect. It's knowing our limits and connecting to the truth that all experiences—even the ones belonging to the little people in our care—are not our experiences.

And that is not easy work.

> *"There are some days we can claim and there are other days that claim us."*
> — Kamand Kojouri

Sometimes surrender in parenting feels like relief, but more often it can feel like torture. Stepping back and letting my no-longer-a-baby climb the jungle gym for the first time was one of my early lessons in surrender. Listening as my oldest son's pediatrician diagnosed him with a visual impairment that meant he might never play sports, ride a bike, or drive a car—feeling all that worry and helplessness—was another part of this daunting practice. Birthing, nursing, boy–girl parties, watching the teenagers suffer heartbreak, sending my oldest child off to college—all these required a type of letting go that felt hard and counterintuitive to nurturing and protecting.

There are joyful lessons of surrender, too. When my oldest left for a college nearly 300 miles away in upstate New York, there was more to consider than what courses to take or meal plan to choose. She also has to deal with a very painful connective tissue disorder that limits her mobility. She requires special accommodations to be able to navigate her dorm and manage the heavy course load of a biology major. Despite the fact that I was there to help her with securing accommodations, she volunteered to take the entire job upon herself. This entailed scheduling meetings with school advocates, filling out all the necessary paperwork, compiling medical records, and explaining her condition to her professors so they could better understand her needs. Once I was willing to let go, she handled it all. That would be a lot for anyone, and I don't know if I would have been able to take on as much as she did as an 18-year-old away from home for the first time, especially with such competence. It was scary to let her take on these big responsibilities, but my heart swelled with pride as I witnessed her tackling each task on her own. My first baby has become an adult woman, and a phenomenal one at that. Beauty emerges when we accept our role as mothers and learn how to use surrender as a tool to nurture and teach—and grow.

We Are All Gardeners

Mothering is not so different than gardening. As a gardener, it's my responsibility to make sure the soil is healthy and viable. Likewise, as a mother, it's important that I take care of my body and keep myself healthy for my family. It's up to me to plant the seeds and water them every day just as I nurture my children daily, providing them with nourishing food, lessons, and affection.

I surrender to Mother Nature to do her part of the job, and I trust my children as they go out into the world, having faith in their deep roots and sturdy stems. And I have to surrender to whatever comes in (both the bad and the amazing), just like with my daughter at college. Because as with a garden, if I am willing to step back, I will watch my children bloom like flowers, offering a beauty all their own. Their beauty is a result of my hard work, but also my surrender.

> *"The garden suggests there might be a place where we can meet nature half way."*
> —Michael Pollan

When I began writing this book, it had been about a year since my oldest son had left home, moving into his father's house and away from me at 17 years old. Our relationship had always had ups and downs, times of closeness and times of emotional strain, but this separation wasn't something I could have predicted. And it sent me into an emotional tailspin.

I had thought I was doing everything (or at least enough) right. How could this be happening to my family? How could I continue to show up in my work when I felt like my own life, or at least a huge part of it, was falling apart? It's always been so important to me to be transparent about my journey, struggles and all.

I almost said no when my publisher asked me to write this book. I looked at my relationship with my son and the shock, confusion, and humiliation it was causing me, and I felt absolutely unqualified to give mothering advice. I mean, how could I teach other women how to parent when I clearly wasn't doing a bang-up job myself?

But what I love most about leading a community of women, most of whom are mothers, is that I get to teach the lessons I most need to learn—whether they are ones I could have used 20 years ago or the ones I am still learning today. In a way, my publisher's request couldn't have been better timed. The Universe always has a funny way of delivering us gifts masked as challenges. Because what I realized as I began to think about this book was that there is no better opportunity to teach a lesson in all its raw and authentic beauty than when we're in the middle of learning it ourselves.

So, I surrendered. I embraced the truth that there simply is no (or very little) "right" or "wrong" in mothering. How many women were experiencing the same self-doubt and pain around their parenting? How many were overwhelmed by their list of things to do, but felt directionless in their efforts? How many of them felt like they were failing? How many of them felt alone? My guess was a lot. And that's all the permission I needed to share my experience.

The Science of Mothering Well

In the following pages, I'll teach you my practical system for building a life you love that allows you to get your to-do list done with ease—without all the yucky stuff like guilt, resentment, and burnout. My system consists of five phases that build upon the wisdom of nature and the work of influential women and teachers who have guided me throughout my 21 years of mothering. The phases also align with one of my core practices in creating more energy in my life. I've lived by and taught this vitality practice for years—ever since I learned it from one of my dearest friends and teachers, Michael Perrine, a certified colon hydrotherapist and holistic health counselor I've worked with extensively to bring nutrition and lifestyle videos to my audience.

In one of our earliest videos, Michael introduced us to the formula $V = P - O$ (Vitality equals Pressure minus Obstruction). In the early 1900s, Professor Arnold Ehret created this formula with dietary practices in mind. As I've come to understand it, vitality in health is achieved when internal obstruction from unhealthy or unnatural foods is removed, allowing for freedom of movement, absorption, and elimination of all external pressure. Translation: when you don't have a pile of gross, indigestible muck sitting in your gut, it's easier for your body to absorb nutrients, digest healthy food, and eliminate toxins.

The system I'm offering you can be applied to every item on your to-do list—big or small. My method is flexible. It will support you in routine tasks—like managing your family's schedule—or creative ones—like mapping your path to a big goal. It's about removing the obstructions in order to handle the pressures with greater ease, so you can have more vitality. Each meditation or stress-management technique I provide in these pages is designed to help you let go of personal drama, anxiety, and tension and create space to contemplate, breathe, and live your life unburdened.

Over the years, I have realized that the most important question in my personal practice is how can I reduce the amount of internal energetic baggage (negative stories, emotions, self-talk, etc.) in order to be free to do the work I love, including being a present and powerful parent. What I have discovered is that when this baggage is cleared out, external stressors move through me much more freely. They don't get trapped in a traffic jam of mental and emotional blocks.

Stress is an inevitable part of life, especially when you're raising a family. Stuff happens—big, out-of-your-control stuff. All the time! Eliminating external stress is not a job you need to add to your to-do list. There is probably no more beautiful a gift to give yourself as a mother than the knowledge that you have the power to be someone who can handle the job with ease and grace (self-love, forgiveness, and surrender to what is). The stories, lessons, and activities in this book are going to allow you to do just that. Expect to do some homework: many of the lessons include short writing assignments. Make sure you have a safe place to record your work and keep it all together—a journal or a spot on your phone or device that only you can access.

I'm going to get *really* real. Expect deeply personal, heartfelt stories about my struggles and tender moments in raising five children to accompany every lesson. And finally, simple guided meditations created specifically for you and this work will seal in the benefits of what you'll be learning in each of the five phases.

Parenting is my most important work, but it's not my only work. Being a mother is part of who I am as a woman, but it's not the only thing that defines me. I want you to come away with a feeling of confidence in finding your own way as a mother and as an independent woman with big dreams and the ability to realize them. Let's shake off the mind-set that we can only accomplish our goals in spite of our tremendous responsibilities as mothers. Because through this system, I have discovered that there is enough time to achieve everything your heart desires *and* still meet the needs of your family. In these pages, I share my favorite healing and stress-management modalities—for you and your loved ones. Upon finishing this book, you will have the know-how to create a path to happiness, freedom, and success that's perfectly aligned with your version of motherhood. No matter what your goal, this method will help you make it happen. And that's coming from someone who's doing it (and still learning) herself.

Phase 1

FERTILE GROUND

CHAPTER 1

ORIGINS OF A PRACTICE

I'll never forget the day my mother taught me how to harness the power and potential of the seasons. Or, rather, my seasons. Over the past 20 years, I've used this practice more than 1,000 times and taught it to others seeking advice. And now it stands at the heart of the program I am sharing with you.

This first time she shared the secret was like any other day in my life at that time. I was living in a modest second-floor Staten Island apartment. I had two young children, and most days would find me sitting on a swivel chair in a small, chilly alcove overlooking the gray street and the yard of a family-run statuary business across the way. A jumbled assortment of Virgin Marys, Buddhas, and concrete animals stared up at me through weeds and a chain-link fence.

I was 21 years old and already the mother of a two-year-old girl and an infant boy. Very few of my friends were in committed relationships, let alone caring for their own children. My family was only an hour's drive across the Goethals Bridge and down the New Jersey Turnpike, but it seemed like an ocean separated us. Instead of connecting with the outside world, I spent hours in that alcove, sitting at the faux-wood desk while my kids played at my feet, trying to escape the mundanity of those long, lonely days. The Internet—filled with message boards, online role-playing games, and early social media platforms like Friendster—was my lifeline to the world.

My landlords controlled the heat, so our apartment was often frigid in the winter. I remember that the day my mom taught me about the seasons was particularly cold. My knees pulled tightly into my chest, I stretched an oversized hooded sweatshirt—probably borrowed from my husband's closet—over my legs and under my toes so every part of my body was covered.

Twenty years ago, long-distance calls on a landline phone weren't cheap—even calls from New York to New Jersey. I was constantly looking for the best deals, negotiating with a new phone company for a lower rate every few months. Finances were lean, but staying in touch with my mother was nonnegotiable. We talked at least half a dozen times every day. My mother and I usually saved long conversations for nights and weekends when we could talk for free, but that day I had serious business to discuss.

Things hadn't been good between my then-husband and myself for a while. For the sake of this story, we'll call him P. I remember that on that particular day I was at the end of my rope, and no amount of organizing toy boxes or disinfecting kitchen surfaces could quiet my anxiety. My mother was always happy to be a receptacle for my stress dumps. She loved commiserating with me about men and her own long history of being the victim of their whims and wrongdoings.

"I can't do this anymore," I cried to her. "We're fighting all the time. I don't want the kids to see this, to end up like this. I want to leave. I want to come home." This conversation was one of a thousand I had with my mother spanning the years of my relationship with my first husband, the father of my oldest children.

P and I were a terrible match. Our relationship was never stable and often abusive, and my anxiety and depression thrived within it. My mother's usual response was to remind me of my responsibility to my young children ("Are you sure you can't work it out for their sake?"). And besides, going home wasn't an option. Though my mother and I loved each other, I left home at 17 with the personal commitment and the maternal directive to stay gone.

The tolerance my mother and I had for each other was tested even further as I matured into a woman. I was creating rules and boundaries for myself, and this often resulted in fights and long estrangements. Although living with my husband was hopelessly difficult and unhealthy, moving in with my mother would have also been unhealthy—just in a different way.

This call was different, though. I'm not sure what inspired my mother's response, but her tone was new. Maybe she fully felt my desperation for the first time. Or maybe it was just because I was finally willing to get real about my marriage. As I would later learn, there are no more powerful factors in good communication than vulnerability and empathy. When we share from a place of radical openness, people are able to feel our experience without all the filters that typically obscure our truths. And in that moment, my mother finally felt mine.

She told me I could leave my husband and that I shouldn't feel ashamed if I did. She pointed out that I had been a teenager when I met P, and that it would be foolish to hold myself hostage to adolescent decisions. Time passes. People grow. And sometimes personal growth requires outside change to support it.

This was nothing like the advice I had heard from her before, so I cut my rant short and got quiet. As my daughter danced back and forth between her princess dolls and fussing with my son, who was strapped snugly into his bouncy seat near the base of my chair, I listened to my mother share details about her past romantic relationships, and how she moved on from each of them—sometimes amicably, but most often painfully—and how this is a natural occurrence in life that shouldn't be judged harshly.

"A lifetime is a long time to be with one person or to expect yourself to stay the same person," she said. "People change, and sometimes that change happens for the better of a relationship. Sometimes it breaks it up. And other times, the change turns the relationship into something new altogether. But just like the seasons, everything changes. It's better to teach yourself to accept that. Resisting change is what is causing you to continue suffering."

My mother's advice allowed me to release the weight that I *thought* was my responsibility—taking care of P and his drama, fixing a broken relationship, creating the perfect family for my children. Though change might be painful, it also precedes growth, progress, success, redemption, and pretty much everything good in life. I had been hurting myself by fighting what was in fact nature's cycle. When things weren't perfect, I blamed and punished myself for it all. Life felt hard because I was in a constant state of resistance. The rigidity I had adopted was transforming into physical stress that showed up as panic attacks, tooth grinding, stomachaches, and fatigue.

My fear of change was suppressing every bit of my own nurturing, growing, blooming, and even breaking down. But on the day I had that conversation with my mother, I learned to see myself as part of nature, too. I wasn't a separate thing, immune to the laws that govern it. I had my own seasons. And they begged to be honored.

I didn't leave my husband the next day (in fact, it would be six more years and another baby before *he* left *me*), but in that moment, I felt the earth shift. I realized that I *could* leave him, and in that moment, the nut cracked open. The seasons changed. It didn't mean life was ending. It meant I was growing.

My Roots

I consider myself very lucky to have grown up in New Jersey. People unfamiliar with the Garden State might picture busy toll roads, rude drivers, and the Sopranos. They're not wrong (I mean, you don't actually see Tony Soprano anywhere, but we know how to make a meatball sandwich). But underneath all the stereotypes, there's actually a lot to love . . . and beauty. My New Jersey has gorgeous mountains and hiking trails, a huge expanse of wild forest called the Pine Barrens (I live on its northern edge), miles of gorgeous beaches, quick access to Philadelphia and New York City, and endless acres of farmland that yield the most delicious produce on the planet.

I inhabit a place that's at once busy and serene, congested and expansive, beautiful and gritty. I, along with my fellow New Jerseyans, embody those same traits. We're a unique people from a unique state. And we have Bruce Springsteen and Bon Jovi (which pretty much tops everything else that I just mentioned). The small factory town of my New Jersey childhood is where I returned to buy my first home before my third child, Jack, was born. And later my new husband, Justin, and I chose an even smaller farming community nearby to settle down in and raise our family.

New Jersey has everything I need, not least being the ability to experience the four seasons in all their incredible (and occasionally terrible) extremes. Each brings its own gifts. Our winters can be rough, but that's how New Jerseyans and our neighbors get our grittiness. What comes off as abrasive and impatient to outsiders is simply an expression of the toughness we've developed in the face of a challenging climate in the most densely populated state in the country. And because of those tough winters, spring is a true celebration of rebirth. The trees come alive with flower blossoms, the birds return with their sweet songs, and bunnies are everywhere! I live for the first warm spring day when I can roll down my car windows and blast the radio as I drive up the parkway to famous Asbury Park for smoothie bowls and tasty local eats—everything from vegan cuisine to classic boardwalk pizza and funnel cake. And then there are our hot, humid, and wonderful summers. Our beaches stretch farther than the eye can see, and summer nights on the boardwalks are what teenage dreams are made of.

But if seasons were love affairs, fall is my true beloved. Our property is eight acres of mostly wooded land. Fall is when Justin starts chopping felled trees for burning in the winter, filling the air with the smell of freshly cut firewood. The leaves do what leaves always do at this time of year—they change.

The forest produces fiery hues that make my eyes dance from tree to tree with delight. This transformation is the most glorious display of decay in nature. Fall is so magical that it makes death beautiful.

"The creation of a thousand forests is in one acorn."
— Ralph Waldo Emerson

The acorns are my favorite part of autumn. Both red and white oak trees are abundant on our property, and they carpet the entire forest floor with their seeds in the fall. It feels like every inch of ground is covered with countless acorns, which are also known as oak nuts (a much cuter name, in my opinion). They come in every shade from yellow to deep auburn. The resident deer delight in snacking on them, but they're not the only ones. Our rescued barn animals love these tasty treats, too. On days when we let them graze outside the barnyard, our dwarf goats and potbellied pigs race from the barn to their grazing paddock and dive into the piles of acorns hidden among the fallen leaves.

I love my animals. If they're not happy, I'm not happy. So, I worry about my farm family while they're cooped up during the cold winter months. One fall, I realized that their favorite autumn snack could also make their winter happier. I had to take action right away! I grabbed some buckets from the barn, rallied my three youngest children (read: bribed them with cash and prizes), and challenged them to fill their metal pails with as many acorns as they could collect in an afternoon. I couldn't wait to clean, roast, and store them for winter. I had to move fast—soon they would be gobbled up by the deer and squirrels, buried in the soil, or smashed to oblivion under the feet of wild animals and children (which can be one and the same).

I didn't intend to take so much time collecting the acorns. We spent hours outside on the first day, and when the children got tired, I stayed to collect more. Over the next several days, I scoured all the corners of our property for the perfect treats for my pets. For every three pails I filled, I would toss one into the barnyard for the gang to enjoy right away. Even the ducks indulged.

Another unintended, or rather unexpected, aspect of collecting acorns was the incredible peace I felt while doing it. My hands were in the dirt, the sights and smells of fall had ignited my senses, and my heart was happy. I collected acorns during the day, and when it got too dark or cold to stay outside, I went inside to my computer, where I researched the different types of oak trees and the life cycles of their seeds. Everything about the process of harvesting, washing, roasting, and researching my acorns reminded me of my mother's lessons about change. We move through life in phases. As I began to pay more attention to my newfound fascination, I discovered that the human life cycle really isn't so different from that of an acorn. We're a lot simpler than we realize.

That fall was particularly rainy, which made the white oak acorns sprout soon after dropping to the ground. The outer shell would crack open, with the sprout reaching outward and into the ground, where it would plant itself. Every time I found another sprouted oak nut, I felt a pang of joy. And it wasn't lost on me that all of this was happening on its own, without my help or input. Not all the acorns were successful. Some would be trampled, some would be gobbled up, and some would be ignored and left behind. But the few surviving would sprout, find the soil, receive perfect nourishment, and succeed in becoming tiny oak trees. If conditions remained good, they would one day tower above us as mighty oaks. And the process would begin again.

Mother Moon

It was just a couple weeks after Mission: Collect All the Acorns when I attended a moon-cycles workshop at a good friend's house. I'd never taken astrology very seriously, but the moon had always been an object of curiosity for me. My mother would celebrate the full moon every month by sitting under twinkle lights in her garden, and later, as she got older, she would serve a special meal on tableware set aside for the event. She was a mystic and a self-proclaimed hippie who listened to New Age music and burned incense in every room. Outside of a few drum circles she dragged me to as a teenager, I was rarely called to join any of her ceremonies. I watched from the outside and, honestly, thought it all kind of strange. But I realize now that—whether it was her intention or not—my mother taught me a valuable lesson about making time for only myself.

Since my mother's passing I've placed some of her belongings around my home, and they still carry the scent of her favorite Nag Champa incense and patchouli oil. My mother's arrival into any room was always preceded by the scent of her patchouli. Sometimes I'll hold one of her treasured objects to my nose to invoke a memory of her. In those moments, I often feel her presence here with me.

"Sooner or later, we all quote our mothers."
— Unknown

As our workshop teacher guided us through the phases of the moon, she referenced parallels in other aspects of nature. Just like the moon waxes and wanes—grows bright, then dims, then disappears into darkness, repeating this cycle in a loop—so goes everything in nature. Something is conceived, it is born, it grows, it peaks, it weakens and decays, and it dies, returning to the soil and replenishing the collective energy of the universe.

As she described this cycle, I saw my acorns in every phase— dropping to the ground, cracking open, and transforming into tiny trees. I recalled a conversation with a friend weeks earlier, when she challenged me to imagine which kind of tree I might be: I told her I saw myself as a slow-growing mighty oak. I thought of my mother, her garden, and her full-moon rituals. I soaked up every word our teacher spoke and contemplated them carefully during our group meditation. I considered what these words meant for me and how they aligned with a practice that I had been applying to my life for years but never named. It felt like all the pieces of my work were falling into place (what a glorious feeling!)—my fascination with cycles in nature, the lessons from my mother, my own desire for rituals to bring me more connection and peace. It all made sense!

I had been using my mother's "seasons" advice for years to ease anxiety, resist the urge to multitask (we'll talk more about that later), and create habits that supported my health and my desire to do *all* the things. Recalling that tiny alcove in Staten Island, where it felt like I was so far away from everything I thought ideal—and which I am living today—my mother's words echoed within me: "Everything has a season. You're no different. You'll change with the seasons just like everything else, and that's okay. There's time for everything you want to do and experience. There's time for everything you need to learn. Don't worry. There's time."

Sure, her words had guided me out of my marriage and into a better life, but I had never thought of it as a practical system that could be used and offered to others.

Immediately, I started translating my experiences into a system to share with my community. And as I worked, I discovered something exciting. I had thought I was creating a productivity tool, but what emerged from my efforts was something different—a tool especially helpful for mothers. For women like me who had hopes and dreams, but also endless to-do lists and big responsibilities. Women who loved being mothers, but ached for the time and mental space to pursue their deepest desires.

This system would be their channel for making those hopes and dreams move from a list to reality. The phone calls with my mother, her lessons about the seasons, memories of her garden, my acorns, and the moon had all been conspiring in the background to bring me to this moment. I realized that I was being called to share my experience as a mother, one who is also successfully pursuing her dreams as an independent, empowered woman. My mission was to show other mothers how by honoring the cycles of Mother Nature, they too could find ease, space, and grace in motherhood. And Managing the Motherload was born.

Let's Make a Pact

I want us to decide something right now, before you read another word. Let's agree that beating yourself up over feeling beat up is silly. It's a waste of time. And it's hurting you and your ability to mother well. There may always be a voice inside you that from time to time tells you that you're not doing enough. And let's face it, the voice usually has a lot more to say than just that. It will insert itself like an unwanted guest into your meditations, in the middle of your workday, and most assuredly, in those last moments before you fall asleep.

If you use the practice I'm about to give you, you can have faith that, that voice will fade over time. Its potency will diminish until it hardly has any effect on you at all. Because no matter how loud or seemingly real that voice is, you have the choice to talk back to it—to offer a different point of view. You can engage with that voice in a way that takes away its power. Speaking truth to that voice will reveal how its message is based on lies. I want you to make a pact with me that you won't allow that voice to have a seat at the table anymore. As soon as it starts flapping its gums and making its butt comfy in your chair, you're going to swipe that chair right out from under it.

> *"I will not let my ICA
> (Inner Asshole) be the boss of me."*
> — Jennifer Pastiloff

Let's face it: your inner voice can be a real asshole sometimes, so don't ever feel bad about shutting it down. I'm going to offer you a complete system for creating an energetic practice that supports your mental and emotional health in the next chapter, but for now, I want to offer a mini-practice that is guaranteed to give you a lot of relief. This three-step mind-set activity is an adaptation of one given to me by my life coach, Lauren Zander, creator of the Handel Method. I incorporate it into my daily morning practice and offer it to my community as the simplest and most profound way to shut down my lying inner a-hole.

STEP 1: NAME YOUR NEGATIVE INNER VOICE.

It's important to give your negative inner voice a name for a couple of reasons. This voice should always be recognized as something separate from you. It is not the essence of who you are, and it certainly isn't reflective of your reality. Giving it a name makes it easier to view it as something outside of you. Naming your negative inner voice also makes it easier to have a conversation with it. Mine is named Becky (and yes, she's totally Becky with the good hair). Please accept my apology if you are or someone you love is a Becky. It just doesn't happen to be my name, and I can't stand it when strangers assign it to me without asking. Every time I hear "Becky," it reminds me of someone rude trying to take up space in my head.

At this point in my practice, it's easy for me to visualize my negative inner voice as one belonging not to me, but to the nagging, gossiping, joy-sucking Becky. And I simply have no time for her nonsense. I have no problem telling Becky where to go without a shred of guilt or self-doubt. Her voice isn't mine. Her words aren't mine. It's easy for me to separate and protect myself from whatever chaos she's trying to stir up. Girl, bye.

STEP 2: JOURNAL ALL THE NEGATIVE MESSAGES.

I've caught a lot of flak for this part. Naysayers have said that it's counterproductive because "what you focus on grows." Well, what do you think happens to something you ignore? It festers and stinks up everything in its vicinity. It dominates your attention and demands your precious time. It demands you cater to it.

Calling out the negative messages in your head by noticing them and writing them down starts to take away their power almost immediately. It nips the drama in the bud, before it grows into an unmanageable weed. Negative thoughts like to stay in the dark inner recesses of our psyches, so let's bring them into the light. No matter how uncomfortable it feels, bringing these messages out into the open, even if it's just you who sees them, is critical to breaking free of their hold.

That's why the second step of this practice is all about getting those negative messages out of your head and onto paper (or in a safe place on your device). Write them down, word for word. This can feel like an uneasy practice at first. You might be taking a full-frontal view of some ugly stuff for the first time. But I promise you it will get easier. I've written things like "You don't have what it takes to be a success. No one takes you seriously because everyone can see what a hot mess you are." And "No wonder your kids can't stand you. They want a mom who stays home and bakes, and you're too busy working on your career and being selfish." Yeah, that still feels gross to write.

But when we shine a light on those negative messages, particularly the gross ones, we reveal just how fragile they are. What's the reason for their fragility? They're not supported by a solid foundation of facts. And much like a vampire that can suck you dry, the voice disintegrates in the light.

STEP 3: TALK BACK WITH FACTS.

This is my favorite step of the practice. It's the one where you get to take the power back from your negative inner voice and speak directly to the lies it's trying to make you believe. You also get to call on all that inner wisdom you've been doubting for too long. You know in your heart what's true, and it's time to let it out! Imagine your negative inner voice, which now has a name assigned to it, as being no different from any other intruder walking into your home unannounced. They are uninvited at best, and downright dangerous at worst—and they need to leave *now*.

You're going to have a lot of fun with this step. The more you do it, the stronger and louder your true voice—that super-mama inner wisdom—will become. If I'm guessing correctly, you're probably already excellent at speaking truth to bullshit. The kind of woman who actively seeks out ways to improve herself is usually the same one who is called upon to give her good advice to others. If only we were more willing to listen to ourselves. Our *true* selves.

Your role in this step is truth-teller. Whatever negative message your inner critic is trying to make you believe, you're going to dismiss it with a few strokes of a pen or taps on a keyboard. You're going to talk back with an accurate accounting of what's actually happening. I'll give you an example from one of my coaching clients, Shayna:

> *Negative Message:* "Stay-at-home moms are better moms than I am.
>
> "Scrolling through Instagram, I see all the stay-at-home moms having so much fun with their children during the day. Playdates are easy to organize and kids are able to have a say in their schedule. Summertime actually means staying at home and sleeping in, and days are filled with a sense of connection that I'm missing out on."

> *Talkback:* "My kids are having fun interacting and socializing with others. They are learning so much at summer camp or in after-school programs—and I am seeing their growth every night when I get home! Time apart does not discount the love we share.
>
> "I work hard to support my family, and my children are learning from my commitment to them. They are watching and mirroring my work ethic and abilities. I can work toward a goal of working from home if that's what I really want, but there is no shame in staying with my outside-the-home job. My children are well cared for, have great friendships, and are having a blast. They are learning lessons and creating their independence and identities while internalizing the core values and examples that they observe from me. When I pick them up, we

have quality time at home, and the weekends are packed with family activities where we all get to be together and connect. I have a special bond with the kids, and no amount of time away during the day can diminish that."

It's that easy to stop a negative message from your own Becky. Name the voice, notice and document the negative message, and talk back with facts. Today, I only document new thoughts. Old, repeating ones stick around for less than a second because that's how quickly I dismiss them. I often find myself thinking, "Becky, we dealt with this already. Step off!" The negative messages are separate from me, and I just don't have space for them anymore.

Mantras to Make the Work Stick

Throughout the book and between each phase, I'm going to offer you affirmative mantras and guided meditations that will help seal in what you're learning as you go. An affirmative mantra is a positive word or phrase that you can repeat silently or out loud for motivation or encouragement or to reinforce your practice whenever you need it. Your affirmative mantra for this practice is:

> *"My thoughts are not who I am. I watch calmly as in and out they flow. I release my thoughts with ease. Out of my head and onto paper they go."*

Get excited—you're already growing! You have two brand-new tools—a three-step mind-set activity and a mantra. Bookmark all the pages that have tools, action steps, mantras, and meditations on them so you can return anytime. Bend corners, mark up the pages using a highlighter, underline your favorite parts, and keep this book in a handy spot. I guarantee it will save you again and again.

Your new practice is a structure that's built to last. Once you learn to integrate the method into your everyday life, you won't be able to revert back to your old ways. Your new way of living will be so powerfully effective that going back to the stress, worry, and overwhelm will be unimaginable. Approach each phase one step at a time and apply the tools and activities where you can in your daily life. It's that simple. You don't have to make drastic changes, because that's not how we grow an oak tree. It's not how we grow children. And it's not how we grow ourselves.

Motherhood is messy. Through this work, we will begin to sort it out. Motherhood can be overwhelming. But we're going to remember to savor its sweet spots . . . and there are so many sweet spots. Motherhood can knock you down, kick your ass, and then make you get up and cook dinner, do the dishes, and get screaming kids to bed. We'll work on learning how to celebrate even those moments (some of the time, at least).

Growing strong roots for your new practice won't be difficult. It always starts with a good foundation, or in terms of the gardening cycle, fertile ground. My fertile ground was cultivated in three ways: a lesson from my mother, a physical practice to support my healthy body, and an energetic/spiritual practice to support a healthy mind-set.

How can I be so confident that this will work for you? Because it works for me. Because I've seen it bloom again and again in the women I've had the honor of accompanying on their journeys. I've watched this method turn around their lives —and not just for a month. This method can be sustained over time, because it becomes a core belief.

A core belief isn't a wish. It isn't blind faith. It's a knowing. It has roots like the oak tree. Together we're going to crack the nut, and we're going to accept that some of our goals aren't going to be achieved, and that that's okay. We're going to learn to surrender to change. And we're going to discover that the more we are willing to release the obstacles in front of us, the less pressure and more vitality we're going to experience. Every day.

CHAPTER 2

PREPARING THE PHYSICAL BODY

Being a mom takes a toll on the body. The minute we get pregnant (and for those who struggle with fertility issues, well before then), we feel the physical strain of motherhood. Making and raising a human is hard work, and there's really no way around that. How we care for our bodies influences the intensity of that hard work and the effect it has on our health and general well-being. But you don't have to grow a baby in your belly to feel the physical strain of motherhood. Adoptive mothers, stepmothers, and all the women who take on the role of mother to another human experience the same sleepless nights, worry, and heartache. They bear the same undereye circles, bruised knees, and aching backs.

The physical stress of nurturing a child can feel overwhelming. I yell. I cry. I get tired. I sometimes spend entire days parenting from the couch, covered in tortilla chip crumbs that I will later fish out of my cleavage. And no, I will not add those crumbs to my daily food diary.

I'm not trying to cast a negative shadow on motherhood, but let's be real. It's messy and exhausting. Adding the pressure of being perfect to an already exhausting task only compounds the exhaustion. It's time we reject the culture our mothers and grandmothers were forced to abide by. We can break the cycle of isolation and pretending everything is just peachy when it's not (or at least not all the time). And we can do that without making it seem like motherhood can't be survived without bottomless cups of coffee and glasses of wine (though I'm not knocking your pumpkin latte or the occasional rosé with your Netflix and chill—you do you, boo). We deserve better than impossibly glossy Instagram accounts that make us feel like hot messes. But a narrative that tells us that motherhood is all about sacrifice and spit-up stains isn't helpful, either. The truth is that motherhood is all those things and so much more—some tough stuff that we can absolutely handle and a lot of beautiful stuff we get to embrace with joy.

Now, let's get back to the business of taking care of your beautiful body. We're going to focus on what I consider the three most important elements of physical health: sleep, diet, and movement. All of my recommendations are appropriate for every stage of motherhood, but please check with your health-care provider before starting any new wellness program or creating a drastic change in your eating or exercise routine.

It's Time for Bed

I'm a little fussy when it comes to sleep. If I don't get a full eight hours, the next day isn't going to be a good one. Now, I'm not saying I always (or really ever) get a completely restful, uninterrupted night's sleep. I don't think that's happened in a nonvacation setting since 1998. So, I make it a general rule to at least *be* in bed for a solid eight hours (minus pee breaks, of course).

Social media is a constant reminder of how motherhood can accelerate the aging process. I remember scrolling through my newsfeed during one of my late-night breastfeeding sessions and seeing an article that featured before and after shots of people who had experienced just one week of moderate sleep deprivation. Honestly, I would have settled for looking as good as the Day 7 "after" pics. Truth: 18 years later, I think I'm still suffering the aftereffects of my first son's colic. And I just got interrupted by my preschooler while typing that last line (it's after midnight). Sleep is, and probably will always remain, a luxury in my eyes.

But before I changed my ways, the long days of chugging caffeine, eating leftovers off my kids' plates, and barely being able to bathe had left me looking like Gollum from the *Lord of the Rings* series. I looked tragic. I felt tragic. And my patience was worn thin before 9 A.M. every day. What made me feel even more hopeless was that the people pictured in the sleep-deprivation article were—hold for the punch line—only getting six hours of sleep per night. Only six hours?! I couldn't even imagine getting six uninterrupted hours of sleep. No chubby-toed karate kicks to the belly at 4 A.M.? No waking up in puddles of freshly dispensed toddler urine? No tiny teeth clamped to one of my nipples to remind me that it's time for the fifth feeding of the night? Six hours was a dream.

So, there I was, tired and feeling woefully unattractive in comparison to my former child-free self. Making up for so much lost sleep seemed hopeless. The icing on the cake was all the warnings about how lack of sleep was not only affecting my attitude and my looks, but also causing years of my life to be lost, too. I was desperate and pissed off and sad. And I looked like a cave creature longing for "my precious" sleep. How was I ever going to fix this?

"I want to be like a caterpillar. Eat a lot. Sleep for a while. Wake up beautiful."
— Unknown

When I confided in my mother about my trouble sleeping, I was still sharing my bed with a nursing baby. "Bedrooms are for two things," my mother said. "Sleeping and making love." A grown woman, I still cringed at hearing my mom say the words "making love." But she went on, "Beds are not for watching TV, eating, or doing work."

She was right, and something had to change. I was already suffering from so many of the negative effects of sustained sleep deprivation—brain fog, irritability, weight gain, and symptoms of depression. Not getting enough sleep can also increase your risk of developing high blood pressure, diabetes, heart disease, a diminished sex drive, a compromised immune system, and premature aging. The list of scary side effects is a mile long.

I started doing a little research, looking for ways to help myself get a better night's rest, and discovered the circadian rhythm, nature's biological "clock." It controls our physical, mental, and behavioral responses to our environment and is primarily influenced by the cycle of light and dark. It became obvious to me that by not making sleep a priority, I was not honoring that rhythm. And being out of rhythm was making me physically and mentally unwell.

I wasn't ready to give up co-sleeping just yet, though, so whatever changes I made would have to be doable with kids still sleeping next to me. Here's what I learned and what you can do to sleep better tonight.

8 PERSONALLY TRIED-AND-TRUE TIPS FOR BETTER SLEEP

1. Sun down, screens off. I'm not trying to take away your #NetflixandChill, but maybe you could try shutting off *most* of your screens once the sun goes down. This will help you wind down earlier and fall asleep faster. Shutting off your screens a little earlier honors your natural circadian rhythm by taking your gaze away from the blue light emitted by electronics. Late-night blue-light exposure has been shown in sleep studies to shorten total sleep time, suppress the production of melatonin (a naturally occurring hormone that aids sleep), and interfere with the quality of sleep by increasing wakefulness throughout the night. If you're not willing to shut down your screens completely, try adjusting the color and brightness levels on your laptop and phone. I use an app that automatically adjusts my phone screen to a warm orange-yellow tint at sunset and then back to normal at sunrise.

2. Set yourself up for sleep success with a sleep-friendly environment. What does that mean? It means keeping your bedroom temperature cool and comfortable, banning anything that buzzes or beeps or lights up (that means your phone, your television, and your laptop), and making your room as dark as you can with blinds or curtains. If you use your phone as your alarm and you aren't able to wake up on your own just yet, try investing in an old-school alarm clock. But turn it so it's facing away from you, so you're not tempted to watch the time if you're having trouble falling asleep (or back to sleep if you wake up during the night).

3. Come up with a bedtime routine that works for you. Think about things that might bring a sense of ease and relaxation, perhaps trying one or more of these suggestions:

- Set a reasonable bedtime that you can stick with regularly so your body will know when you're expecting to sleep.

- Take a warm bath.

- Write in a journal so you can unload all the day's stressors before your head hits the pillow. Remember the mantra I offered you at the end of the previous chapter, "Out of my head and onto paper they go." Keep the journal handy on your nightstand.

- Read or listen to a book or listen to music. Books that are a little dull or don't challenge you to think too much work wonders.

- Do some nice, easy stretching or yoga right in bed.

- Have sex or engage in self-pleasure. Orgasms are fantastic for stress relief.

- Try a sleep-specific meditation when you're ready to hit the hay. I have lots of yoga- and meditation-for-sleep videos for you at YouTube .com/BexLife.

4. Watch what you eat and drink close to bedtime. If you eat a late dinner or feel the need for a snack, make sure you finish eating at least one to two hours before your bedtime. All the work that goes into digesting your food can take away from your body's ability to rest and repair while you're sleeping. This goes for alcohol, too—drink it too close to bedtime and you'll be sorry. I know the "nightcap" you enjoy before bed feels like it's relaxing you (and it might be), but the truth is that too much alcohol actually disrupts your sleep. Keep yourself to a one-drink maximum.

5. Keep an eye on high-octane stimulants. I'm a huge advocate for going caffeine-free, but if you feel like caffeine works for you, I won't make you give it up. However, I would suggest sticking to one or two cups of coffee—or even high-voltage tea—in the morning. If you have more than that or bring caffeinated drinks into your afternoon, you're asking for trouble at bedtime; your body won't be able to shut off and get the sleep it needs. Try some decaf herbal teas in the afternoon and when you're winding down at night. Both passionflower and chamomile teas are popular and easy to find and can promote a good night's sleep. But anything that has a calming effect and doesn't contain sugar or caffeine is a great option.

6. Give a melatonin supplement a try. Melatonin is a little different from your average sleep aid on the pharmacy shelves because it is produced naturally by your brain to bring about a regular sleep cycle (your natural melatonin levels are generally higher at night). Unlike sleeping pills, melatonin won't knock you out or give you that fuzzy hangover feeling the next morning. The best thing about it is that because it doesn't cause any sort of dependency, it's not habit-forming. That said, you should first talk to your doctor or pharmacist to see if it's right for you, and only take it on a short-term basis.

7. Go all natural with essential oils. Aromatherapy can help with a lot of nuisances in your life, and sleep issues are no exception. Among the many ways you can use them: place them in a diffuser to release their scent into your living room or bedroom, or add them to your bath water if hopping in the tub is part of your nighttime routine. Some oils can even be dabbed directly on your skin (check the instructions to be sure it's safe), or you can sprinkle the oils on an eye pillow or sleep mask for sweet dreams. I love lavender in particular, especially right on the pillow, but ylang-ylang (also a natural aphrodisiac), bergamot, and sandalwood are also great bedtime oils.

8. Plug into some binaural beats. You've probably heard of Beats by Dre, but binaural beats may be a totally foreign concept to you. These sound waves can help your brain reach a state very similar to meditation quickly and easily. There are a variety of different wave patterns that you can listen to in order to achieve a specific goal (focus, clarity, or stress relief, for example), but the right binaural beats can encourage your brain to relax into a sleep-ready state. Search for a free binaural beats app; I use one that combines beats with sounds of nature and also gives you the option to upload a playlist of your favorite soothing songs. Though you shouldn't have phones on your bedside table, you can listen to the app before moving the phone to another room. If you find it extra-helpful for drifting off and would rather keep the phone with you, at least make sure you set your phone to airplane mode so you won't undo your progress by waking up at 3 A.M. to a Facebook notification.

I chose sleep as the first part of physical health to discuss because it's often the most overlooked. Surveys of primary care physicians have revealed that many of them—up to 60 percent—don't even ask their patients about their sleep habits. Too many of us place sleep low on our priority list (if it's even on the list) and brag about how well we operate when we're not getting enough of it. Not sleeping has become a badge of honor, when really it's a dangerous and depressing habit. Mistakenly, we think that as mothers, it's self-indulgent to take the time to get the rest we need. We're supposed to be up all night and still operate like superwomen, right?

I personally don't ever want to win a contest for being the most worn out. I want to feel alive and ready to take on every day. I want to leap out of bed, excited about what the Universe (and my gang of tiny humans) has in store for me. So, I sleep like my life and happiness (as well as my family's) depend on it. Are you ready for your nap? I'm going to guess yes.

Eating for Vitality

I'm a total brat when it comes to dieting, so I don't do it. Unless something is going to make me physically sick (gluten, mangoes, dairy), I'm probably going to eat it. And truth be told, I've set aside the discomfort of a mild allergic reaction to eat a perfectly ripe mango more times than I can count. Luckily for me and a lot of women like me who suffer from food sensitivities, gluten- and dairy-free options are easy to find, and they no longer have to cost a *whole* paycheck (if you know what I mean). Good health has gone mainstream, so even big-box discount stores now carry organic foods at a fraction of what they used to cost.

Nutritious, wholesome foods should be enjoyed in abundance, and if there's anything I'm decidedly not into, it's deprivation. But while I'm not about deprivation, I do think there are certain so-called foods that aren't ideal for human consumption. (You'll see a lot of those foods on the "Foods to Avoid" list on page 29.)

> *"I don't mean to brag, but I finished my 14-day diet in 3 hours and 12 minutes."*
> — Unknown

I strive for healthy, easy, normal eating. And dieting isn't normal. Most diets are meant to be merely a temporary departure from how you regularly eat. They often involve complicated or strict guidelines, and many aren't sustainable over a long period of time. Also, dieting can be taxing on your physical and mental states. As Ellyn Satter, a registered dietitian, a family therapist, and an internationally recognized authority on eating and feeding, explains, you should eat when you're hungry, and stop when you're satisfied. But, she says, give yourself room to overeat—or undereat—at times, even if it's just because of how good (or bad) the food tastes. Approach eating with a relaxed attitude and don't be restrictive; have the foods you love, even the ones whose nutritional value is suspect. Pay attention to your food choices and strive for healthy meals, but don't let food become an obsession that takes up all of your attention or time or makes you feel guilty or deprived. Trust your body to know what it needs to function optimally, and listen to what it tells you. Enjoy food! Just be mindful of what and how much you're eating, and try not to overdo it. Paying attention will pay off in better health.

What mom wants to have *less* energy while making her routine *more* complicated? The way to feel sustained vitality is to create a consistent eating routine that supports you every day. Let's go back to the concept I was telling you about in the Introduction, V = P − O (Vitality equals Pressure minus Obstruction). This formula lays the foundation for the simplest method of eating I've ever come across, a plan crafted by my friend Michael Perrine. It's the one I use every day to manage my own health, and it's easy to follow—you just remove any obstruction to allow your body to digest and move the resulting waste through you as efficiently as possible. What follows are some of the basics.

5 TIPS FOR INCREASED VITALITY

These tips allow you to be gentle on your body and your digestive system by moving from light to heavier foods as the day progresses. Don't feel like you have to follow any of these tips strictly. They're just tips—there are no rules here.

1. Eat fruit alone (or with greens). Fruit sugar will ferment into alcohol and gas if its passage through the digestive system is slowed down. This can cause serious bloating and discomfort, so enjoy an abundance of delicious sweet fruit on its own.

2. Start light, then go heavier throughout the day. Fruits and raw juices first, then vegetables, followed by starches and fats next, leaving proteins for the end of the day (or at the end of a meal if you're combining multiple food groups at one mealtime).

3. Nix the late-night meals. Eating late at night means having a full tummy in the morning. After a starch- or protein-heavy dinner, stick to yummy caffeine-free teas or liquids before bedtime.

4. Avoid mixing starches and proteins in the same meal. They compete for the body's digestive enzymes, leaving you with less energy and incomplete digestion. If you like to mix these food groups, remember to take your time while eating—chew and enjoy each bite fully. Letting your teeth and saliva do the mashing and pre-digesting takes a load off your digestive tract. Slow eating makes for a happier belly!

5. Give your belly a break. You don't need to eat all day. Allow 4 to 6 hours between meals and 12 to 14 hours overnight to allow the periods of emptiness required for your body to digest and detox. Also, opt for whole foods instead of complicated meals and snacks. Whole foods, water, and rest are your best friends.

I realize that even with these guidelines, it can be hard to figure out what to eat and what to avoid. Here are general lists of foods to avoid and foods to enjoy, as offered by Kasey J. Smith, a mother of three, postpartum doula, and holistic health coach certified by the Institute for Integrative Nutrition who specializes in prenatal health and postpartum recovery. (To get a free 7-day meal plan from Kasey as part of my 21-Day Soul Cleanse, be sure to claim your bonus gifts at BexLife.com/book.)

Foods to Avoid (or to Use in Moderation—No Deprivation!)	Foods to Enjoy
Gluten (found in wheat, barley, and rye, as well as many processed foods) **Dairy** **Meat** (beef, pork, poultry, and seafood) **Soy** (except miso, tamari, and tempeh) **Caffeine** **Sugar** **Soda and diet soda** **Alcohol** **Artificial ingredients** (colors, flavors, preservatives) **Artificial sweeteners** (aspartame, sucralose, acesulfame potassium, saccharin) **Processed foods** **Butter and butter substitutes** (margarine, Earth Balance, etc.) **Canola and soybean oils** (aka "vegetable oil") **Monosodium glutamate** (MSG; food additive) **Regular soy sauce** (contains gluten; choose tamari or gluten-free soy sauce) **Unrefrigerated bottled dressings** (contain chemicals, sugar, and preservatives) **HFCS** (high-fructose corn syrup), corn syrup, and corn sugar **Table salt** (devoid of nutrients)	**All vegetables** (fresh or frozen) **All fruits** (fresh or frozen) **Gluten-free grains** (oats, rice, quinoa, millet, amaranth) **Beans and legumes** (black beans, lentils, chickpeas, etc.) **Nuts and seeds** **Dairy-free milks** (almond, cashew, coconut, rice, hemp, hazelnut, etc.) **Dairy-free yogurts** (preferably unsweetened or lightly sweetened) **Healthy fats** (coconut oil, coconut butter, extra-virgin olive oil, grapeseed oil, avocados, nuts, and seeds) **Eggs** **Corn chips** (blue or yellow), corn and gluten-free tortillas, root veggie chips **Natural sweeteners** (Stevia, monk fruit extract, honey, pure maple syrup, agave) **Superfoods** (maca, cacao, goji berries, chia seeds, spirulina, etc.) **Herbs and spices** **Sea salt, kosher salt, pink Himalayan salt, etc.** (full of trace minerals) **Herbal teas** (chamomile, dandelion, rooibos, etc.) **Unsweetened sparkling water or mineral water** (great as a soda substitute)

I want to reiterate how important it is to find an eating routine that works for you. If you have a tight budget or you live in an area where access to certain foods is limited, you can only work with what you've got. Be easy on yourself and do the best you can. No plan is one-size-fits-all. The methods and lists in this chapter are only general guidelines for managing your vitality, and even following just a few of the suggestions will give you noticable results. Before making any big changes to your diet, though, be sure to get the okay from a qualified health professional, and check in with them regularly about how you're feeling to make sure you're fueling your body well.

For so many of us, food is tied to our emotions, and doing the work to disconnect it from our childhoods, our traumas, and even our addictions can be tough. But the more we can see food as fuel for our bodies as opposed to an emotional relationship, the better we can develop healthy and normal eating habits. For some of us, this work is a simple process, but no matter where you are with your relationship to food, there is hope. This doesn't mean that food can't or shouldn't feel good. One of my favorite ways to celebrate my mother's memory is by sharing a Jewish apple cake, her most delicious dessert recipe, with my kids. But by minimizing our emotional attachment to food, we make more emotional room for all the other important relationships in our lives.

Your Body in Motion

There was a time when I liked going to the gym four times every week for three hours at a time. I wasn't an athletic kid, so finding fitness after having three babies felt exciting and empowering. I went full-tilt into a healthy, fit lifestyle—working out with heavy weights, running races, and becoming a fitness trainer and yoga teacher. My reluctant husband, the proud owner of a "dad bod," even came along for the ride. The compliments on my "new" body felt great, but the pace wasn't sustainable. I burned out physically, and that did a number on me mentally. I also started falling back into the trap of measuring my self-worth on the way I looked. It didn't feel good, but I continued because the praise and attention made it feel right.

Soon, I found out my fourth baby was on the way, and I continued to teach yoga throughout the entire pregnancy. Then, a series of life-altering events derailed everything. In the span of less than three years, I lost three parents. My stepfather died in early 2011, right before I gave birth, and I lost both my father and my mother in 2013. Another pregnancy, my fifth baby, came only a month after my mother died. The wild cycle of birth and death, joy and loss, as well as physical and mental strain left me feeling untethered and without any will to continue taking care of myself. I gained nearly 30 pounds and felt like a failure.

"If you are in a bad mood, go for a walk. If you are still in a bad mood, go for another walk."
— Hippocrates

That was then. Today, I've found a way to accept my body as it is. The truth is that I haven't stepped into a gym in years, and I'm totally fine with that. I've created a gentle, fun, and supportive way to approach fitness that places the focus on how I feel rather than how I look. My exercise routine consists of much gentler yoga, brisk walks, and sprints up and down the stairs with laundry baskets rather than free weights and races. I feel good in my body and in the knowledge that loving who I am doesn't require hard work. And that feels like pure freedom. You might love Pilates, doing workouts at a box gym, or recruiting local moms for a running club—whatever works for you is exactly what you should do. Try something new and let yourself be surprised by how much you love moving your body. I've been secretly dying to throw on some neon Hammer pants and take a Zumba class at my local YMCA. Maybe declaring it here will make that happen!

Becoming a Friend to My Body as She Is

I'm done telling women how to exercise. The way you choose to move your body should be personal to you and should support your individual goals. It should feel good. What I do want to offer are the valuable tips and lessons I learned on the way to accepting my body as she is in every moment. I hope that you are able to use the following statements to guide you toward movement that feels supportive, nourishing, and kind to your body. Jot them down in a journal or on sticky notes and use them like the loving mantras I mentioned earlier.

I refer to my body as "she/her" instead of "it." This practice reinforces my positive and deeply spiritual relationship with her. My body deserves my love and respect. I work in collaboration with her as my friend.

My body would never betray me. Feelings of betrayal stem from a made-up story. She merely operates in response to her environment and the way I care for her. When I judge my body harshly, it hurts her. I choose to motivate her with kind words and helpful actions.

I replace a goal weight with a goal *feeling*. I focus on how I want to feel in my body, and I make decisions that will take me closer to that feeling. Feeling healthy is more important than appearing healthy.

Wearing clothes that fit is self-care. I'm no longer putting off treating myself to clothes I like because I'm a certain size or *not* a certain size. And I've also stopped trying to squeeze myself into clothes that I've outgrown. It's physically uncomfortable and demoralizing. Buying a size up in my favorite jeans instead of having to become a contortionist in order to zip up the old pair is an act of self-love. I dress my body like the goddess she is.

My health journey isn't one I have to navigate alone. I call on buddies to hold me accountable and to lovingly cheer me on along the way.

I honor the ebb and flow of available energy. I don't push myself beyond my limits physically, mentally, or emotionally. I refuse to hurt myself in the process of maintaining my health. I move in a way that feels good and fun!

I honor my changing shape, always. Every stage of mother-hood requires something different from my body. I allow her to expand, shrink, move, and rest accordingly.

My body is never lost to me. I reject the language of "getting my body back." She is always here, supporting me as a good and faithful friend.

How did those statements feel when you read them? Did they feel true for you? Uncomfortable? If they didn't feel good right away, try leaning in and sitting with them for a bit. This is another part of the journey that requires surrender. Take time to imagine and consider another way. Adopting even just a few of those statements as part of your inner knowing will allow you to create a movement routine that works for you.

Take Action

Use this space to list three changes or "upgrades" you'd like to make in each of the following categories over the next week. An upgrade doesn't have to be a huge, sweeping change. It can be as small as using less sugar in your coffee or going to bed 15 minutes earlier. Small changes add up to a lot. Acknowledge that fact and let yourself feel good about every step—big or small—that you take toward progress.

Sleep

1. _____

_____

2. _____

_____

3. _____

_____

Eat

1. _____

_____

2. _____

_____

3. _____

_____

Move

1. _____

_____

2. _____

_____

3. _____

_____

Bookmark this page to remind yourself of the loving practice that is managing the motherload. If you don't get to everything on the list right away, don't sweat it. Your list will be here to remind you of the little changes you can make when you're ready to make them. This is how real and lasting change happens. Grand gestures can feel amazing—for a little while. But it doesn't take long for the fatigue of overdoing it to set in. "Go big or go home" can't apply to self-care. That's the opposite of grace. I say, give yourself permission to go small, and feel at home—safe, comfortable, and at peace—with every step you take in your self-care. Nourish yourself with action steps centered in kindness.

CHAPTER 3

PREPARING THE ENERGETIC BODY

Children don't stretch just our bodies. They stretch our hearts, too. Motherhood is a physical and mental undertaking like no other. No matter how you came to be a mother, in order to raise up a little one, you pay with body, mind, and spirit. The good health of all three of these aspects of womanhood is integral to a positive mothering experience. Running on empty in just one area affects all areas. In the last chapter, I guided you through ways to better care for your physical body. Now I want to help you create a practice that supports your energetic body—your mental and spiritual well-being.

This chapter is not about creating a state of perfect, unwavering bliss. I don't know if that's even possible, and it definitely isn't in the midst of living with children. This book is about managing a sometimes (or oftentimes) super-stressful existence. Because I think we can all agree—kids can be the worst! They can suck your time, your energy, and your spirit dry, and not even apologize for it. And then they grow up and blame you. It's a good time for all. I'm not ashamed to say that there are days when I just need to lock the door and cry myself through a breathing exercise. I might have written a book on meditation, but I have also angry-meditated *a lot*. And even though I don't recommend it, it still kind of works. Look, this mama is going to access her peace and calm by any means necessary!

Waiting until you've reached your limit to take care of your emotional state is no way to live. How does that saying go? An ounce of prevention is worth a pound of cure? In my first book, *You Have 4 Minutes to Change Your Life*, I showed how creating and maintaining a short but deeply meaningful and effective meditation practice can support you through all of life's bumps, big and small. Daily meditation is not only the foundation of my mothering practice, it's also the foundation for every bit of success and happiness I enjoy today. It's how I can laugh when my toddler walks into the room with every inch of her covered in permanent marker, Vaseline, and maxi pads. It's how I hold together the pieces of my broken heart when my teenager screams, "I hate you!" My daily practice allows me to roll with the punches and surrender to what is.

I discovered meditation when I was just 15 years old. My mother was working at her good friend's used bookstore, and she tasked me with helping her pack up in preparation for the store's move to a new location down the street. When I've told this story in the past, I say that I found a copy of Ram Dass's *Be Here Now* on the shelf and felt that I needed it so badly that I stole it. Today, I have come to believe that the book stole me. It called to my heart and asked me to take it home. What I found in its pages changed my life.

For the first time, I became aware of a spiritual practice that turned my attention inward, rather than focusing outward, like when I prayed to God. Through meditation, I was taught to trust and honor my inner wisdom. It was during a time in my life where I was plagued by severe anxiety and depressive thoughts. I felt insecure and out of control, and I was desperate for relief. I was drowning in adolescent turmoil, feeling like everyone else was making decisions for me, and bad ones, at that. By carefully studying the messages in *Be Here Now*, I slowly started to cultivate a sense of ownership over my experience. I began practicing my own makeshift version of meditation—finding a quiet spot and asking myself what I thought the messages meant—and realized that I had the power to change what I didn't like about my life. My meditation practice made me feel safe and powerful and in control. It still does that for me today, and that's why sharing the transformative and healing power of meditation has become one of the biggest parts of my life's mission.

Meditation Is for You, Too

Let me offer you my personal definition of meditation, which I shared in my first book:

> *"Yes, I see you. I recognize that you're a thinking, feeling person, and I'm here to listen." That's the essence and magic of meditation—the gift of telling yourself that you matter and that you're worth time and attention. No pomp. No circumstance. No rules. Just showing up for yourself with compassion and without judgment. When this is your practice, meditation can serve as a mirror and the lighthouse that leads you home.*

Since I've already written a whole book on meditation and posted scores of instructional videos on YouTube in which I guide the viewer through meditations on every topic imaginable, I'm just going to give you the basics here. You're a busy mom, and I know you need something easy you can do now.

Here's what you need to get started with a perfect meditation practice:

Relative quiet. "Relative" being the operative word. I've meditated plenty of times to the sounds of tiny hands jiggling a doorknob and kids fighting to the brink of death over an iPad. You'll notice quickly that a common theme in this book is "do what you can, when you can, with what you've got." If I had to wait for perfect quiet to do *anything*, I'd get nothing done. I certainly wouldn't have time for Netflix binges, or even writing this book.

Your breath. Can you inhale and exhale? Awesome! You're practically a meditation pro. Just taking the time to get quiet, close your eyes, and focus your attention on your natural inhales and exhales is a perfect meditation practice in action. You'll learn how using simple "distractions" like following your breath or repeating an affirmation can help you to focus quickly. It's why counting sheep is one of the simplest and best ways to fall asleep: when you focus your attention on something mundane and repetitive, it distracts you from stressful thoughts that might be keeping you awake.

Your bottom. Checking in with yourself can be done in any moment, in any position, but sitting upright or reclined during your time in meditation is better than standing. You don't have to be perfectly relaxed to experience a good meditation session, but it's better to be comfortable. My favorite meditation position is sitting upright, my legs crossed, on a small pillow on the floor. But I've also been known to meditate in my laundry room and my bathroom, in my car in the driveway and parking lots, and tucked away in corners at parties. When I need a time-out, I take it.

> *"Mindfulness isn't difficult, we just need to remember to do it."*
> — Sharon Salzberg

In order to get the most out of meditation, here is what I hope you let go of before beginning your practice:

The idea that meditation is about thinking about nothing, that it takes a lot of time, or that you have to be a deeply spiritual person to experience its benefits. You have a lot on your mind, and you're probably a master multitasker just by virtue of the fact that you're a mom. You've developed these superhuman skills because you're busy and have a lot on your plate. Making time for yourself might feel daunting at best, and selfish at worst. You would describe yourself as a spiritual person, but most of the time you just need a little help getting through the regular stress of the day. You don't need it to be deep or complicated. None of that will make you a bad meditator, I promise. I'm going to lead you through easy cues to help you settle into a meditation practice in which you'll be able to focus and feel relaxed at the same time. It won't take long to feel the effects. And with time, you'll streamline your technique and enjoy even greater benefits. Every session will build on the last. Your intuition will grow stronger, and making better, more loving choices about your own physical, mental, and emotional health will become automatic and easy.

The worry that if it doesn't feel awesome, you must be doing it wrong. Comfort zones are great. How exquisitely stunning do we look when we're doing something we know how to do perfectly? Prancing around in our comfort zones is wonderful for stroking the ego, but not so much for growing and evolving. Stumbling, failing, and even falling flat on your face are all proof that you're doing something right. Meditation, success, and enlightenment are a lot like the ocean. Chances are that even the greatest achiever in any of these is probably just dipping their toes in the water. Okay, maybe they've made it in up to their knees. But no matter where you are in your process, remember the wise words of Dory: "Just keep swimming."

Any other preconceived notions about how a wellness, spiritual, or mothering journey should look. As you uncover, discover, go deep, grow, emerge, and bloom, things might get messy. Like a lotus that finds her way through the muck and mud to the sunlight, and a tiny acorn that pushes its path through the dirt and cracks open to eventually grow into a mighty oak, so, too, will you find your way through darkness, stress, and uncertainty to your light. Evolution of mind, heart, and body isn't always pretty, and it doesn't always feel good. Sometimes it hurts. Pretty much like motherhood! But the discomfort—that pressure—is always in service to bringing forth something even more beautiful. With every growing pain, you get closer to birthing the miracle that is a more vibrant, truthful, gorgeous you. Bringing a new life forward is courageous. It takes power. It takes belief. It takes support. I hold that power and belief and support for you. Transformation is not just possible, it's vital. Nothing alive stays the same. Open yourself to welcoming new seasons, new cycles, and the acts of letting go and receiving. Go ahead and surrender to the pressure, and push, and grow!

Training Your Intuition

Meditation is simply about taking the time to connect to yourself and your intuition. We all start out as pretty confident, brave beings. Think about a toddler taking her first steps. No matter how many times she falls down, she gets up and tries again. She knows that she must learn to walk. Success is predetermined. Over time, because of hurtful experiences, other people's negative opinions, or just the general scary stuff in our outside world, we begin to feel small or out of control. We start to lose faith in our ability. We stop trusting our intuition. Not having a strong belief in intuition or inner wisdom can make motherhood feel even harder.

A good meditation practice not only puts you in touch with your intuition, but also helps to strengthen it. Let me explain. Imagine a little girl sitting in a classroom. She's young, maybe five years old, and this is her first experience at "big kid" school. The teacher asks the class a question, and a dozen tiny hands shoot straight up into the air. Remember, little kids come equipped with loads of self-confidence. The teacher calls on the little girl, and she immediately blurts out a very loud but also very wrong answer. All of the other kids giggle at her mistake, and the teacher shakes her head in disapproval, moving on to the next little kid with a raised hand. The little girl feels embarrassed and defeated.

What do you think will happen the next time the teacher asks the classroom to volunteer an answer to a hard question? The little girl might raise her hand but probably with a little reluctance, a little more slowly, and only for questions she's sure she can answer correctly. Maybe the embarrassment of being wrong was too much for her to take and she won't answer at all. Receiving outside encouragement is important when learning something new. When toddlers are learning to walk, we cheer them on and clap with delight at every step. And when they fall, we scoop them up to offer reassuring hugs and kisses. You see, we hold their success in our hearts and minds as a predetermined thing, too. We would never say, "Silly toddler, just give up. Walking is not for you." That would be ridiculous and cruel.

Now, think of your intuition as being that little girl. Imagine that every time you get a gut feeling or a pang of insight, you nurture it with curiosity instead of judgment and dismissal. How would the outcome for the little girl be different if the teacher responded to her wrong answer with "Hmmm, interesting. Tell me how you came up with that answer." The little girl would feel heard and respected. She would engage and tell more. And even if she wasn't sure if her answer was right, she would raise her hand again and again. Your intuition is a little girl speaking to you. It might not always be right on the money but getting curious about its message will reveal a greater truth. You'll also train your intuition to be louder and to raise its hand faster. You'll develop a relationship with your intuition based on trust and respect. Too often we dismiss our gut feelings and instead make other people's opinions or conventional wisdom the superior guiding force in our lives. Do you see how that can be disastrous in motherhood?

Before Mommy Wars

My oldest child was born in 1998, only a few years after the Internet as we know it was invented. I got my first computer and an AOL account when she was just shy of a year old. The clunky beige desktop computer lived in the kitchen of my tiny New York apartment, where it was plugged into the phone line for a dial-up connection. I would nurse my daughter on my lap while searching for random facts with the help of Ask Jeeves, one of many pre-Google search engines. Message boards were a prototype of social media, and I was having fun as an early adopter, learning how to code in HTML and building my first primitive webpages on sites like gURLpages and GeoCities. The Internet felt fun and safe.

It doesn't feel quite like that anymore. Social media has replaced message boards. We interact with friends (and strangers), shop, and get our news all in the same place. We debate social issues and politics with a fierceness and candor that we probably would never express in a real-life encounter. And we offer up our private lives for comment, criticism, and clicks of the like button (or some love/laugh/angry-face variation). Social media can be fun, educational, and life enhancing, but it can also be isolating and scary—especially for moms.

I feel lucky to have started my mothering journey before social media was a thing. All my so-called mistakes were made in private, witnessed by only supportive friends and family. At times when I felt unsure of myself, I had a reassuring place to land within the compassionate feedback and sometimes commiseration of my mother and girlfriends. It wasn't until I started spending a lot of time online that I started doubting myself as a mother—well, the kind of doubt that made me question whether I should even be allowed to raise my own children. My mess-ups felt so big in comparison to the glossy version of motherhood I saw in my social media feeds. And I already had three children by then!

"Comparison is an act of violence against the self."
— Iyanla Vanzant

Once parenting opinions and advice started piling up online, I learned very quickly that everything I was doing was ruining my kids for life. Raising my voice was traumatizing them, as was being too permissive. Co-sleeping would make my kids dependent and needy. And every product in every cabinet in my house was toxic and needed to be thrown out and replaced

NOW. I breastfed for *far* too long, and sending my kids to public school was a lazy decision that was sure to lower their IQs. On the other hand, homeschooling would make them social outcasts. Also, essential oils were magical, which invariably led to "Can I inbox you about a super-amazing opportunity that I know you'd be perfect for?" Everything I was doing as a mother was wrong, but also way righter than that lady who let her kids ride their bikes to the park by themselves! Or was that a good thing? Who knows? Figuring out how to raise my kids required constantly pitting my intuition against the noise of the outside world that was flooding my brain through the computer screen. I needed my meditation practice more than ever.

I had become that little girl who raised her hand and got shot down again and again. I lost confidence in my ability to make the correct decisions for my kids, and I was constantly on the defensive against well-meaning strangers who felt it was their duty to show me how to be a better mother. It was exhausting. And I saw other mothers in my community suffering from the same lack of confidence. We crave the community and connection to the outside world that social media offers, but it's no fun feeling as if your abilities are constantly under attack— either from other people you've never met before or from your own negative inner voice that thrives on comparison. There are no winners in the mommy wars. They produce only casualties. So, what can you do to protect yourself?

Meditation is the best way I've found to strengthen my intuition and build self-confidence. In quiet moments, I allow myself to check in and pull forward worries, doubts, and even big ideas that I've pushed aside as nonpriorities during busy days. I tell myself that my heart knows best. I ask myself questions, wait for my inner wisdom to raise her hand, and then listen with compassion and curiosity—never judgment. I use affirmations to reinforce what I hear from within, and to create a shield of protection from unwelcome criticism.

When other people make me question myself as a mother, I use meditation to tune in to what I know to be true. Meditation is how I practice being a friend to myself. I lean on my girlfriends a lot, especially in the wake of the separation with my son, but there are also moments when I call upon myself to be that friend. I take the time to sort through my feelings one by one and soothe my aching heart, just like I would for my best friend. I reassure myself by focusing on messages of loving support, and I remind myself that I'm doing my best with what I have (and that my best is pretty good).

How to Create a Meditation Space of Your Own

Step one in creating a meditation practice is setting aside the time and space to make meditation happen, and I promise that isn't hard to do. Because being able to de-stress and manage my anxiety is critical to my health, I created a meditation practice that can be done anywhere and be effective in as little as four minutes. With five kids in the house, there isn't much space or uninterrupted time to take for myself (peeing alone is a major victory), so I had to get creative. I'm lucky to have three meditation spaces in my home—two inside, and one outside in the backyard. Don't worry if you don't think you have a space to carve out just for meditation. No matter what your living space looks like, it's easy to create a special place for your practice.

5 ELEMENTS OF A PERFECTLY PEACEFUL SPACE

1. Doors that shut. I said earlier that total peace and quiet isn't always realistic, but meditation is a practice of self-care that should be honored as something special meant just for you. It's okay to disengage and take time for yourself. And it's okay to set proper boundaries and expectations regarding that time. Setting aside a dedicated room for meditation probably isn't realistic in a home with children, but setting up space *inside* a room is doable for almost anyone. My indoor meditation spots are in my laundry room and my bedroom, both places where I can shut the door. I tell my family when I need to take time for myself and that I expect them to respect it. The kids still come a-knockin', but I'm not answering (while deep in meditation). They always get their mom back, and a happier version at that. The extra benefit is that my kids learn how to set boundaries for their own private spaces. My seven-year-old isn't shy about demanding a time-out, going to his bedroom, and shutting the door behind him. And we respect that boundary by waiting to talk to him until he comes out.

2. Soothing colors. I prefer cool colors like sky blue for relaxation spaces (like my bedroom) and bright, cheery colors for work spaces (like my laundry room and office). If I meditate at any time other than morning or before bed, it's usually to center myself quickly and get motivated for the next part of the day. My laundry room, sunny and painted sunflower yellow, is the perfect spot for a midday pick-me-up meditation. If painting a whole room is too big an undertaking, decorate with textiles in your favorite colors.

3. A few of your favorite things. Meditation "altars" have become very popular. You can search Pinterest for hundreds of ideas on how to decorate your space. I keep little figurines of my favorite childhood heroines—Wonder Woman, fitness Smurfette, and Glinda the Good Witch—in my laundry room. Other special places in my home are decorated with feathers collected from my farm birds, artwork made by good friends, crystals from a shop I used to visit with my mother, and souvenirs from romantic vacations or trips to flea markets with my husband. Most of the objects were free or inexpensive, but they're unique and beautiful to me. They all make my heart smile, and that's the only criterion for making the cut.

4. Natural beauty. I live on an eight-acre farm, so it's easy for me to find space outside that's away from people. Soon after we moved to our property, my husband and I dismantled an old deer fence and upcycled some of the wood into a meditation platform for me and a jungle gym for our dwarf goats. If you're tight on outdoor space, try bringing the outside in with easy-to-care-for houseplants. (I follow TheJungalow on Instagram for gorgeous nature-driven decorating inspiration.) Decks, porches, rooftops, and balconies are all ideal outdoor meditation spots, too. But just sitting next to an open window where you can enjoy the sunlight and sounds of nature is perfectly adequate.

I don't mind the soundscape of a bustling city. If you listen intently enough, you'll notice how the sounds of a busy street can turn into rhythmic music to your ears. But natural beauty doesn't mean only the sounds found outside. Just this morning, I heard my two littlest kids telling each other about the dreams they had last night. Their sweet voices were the perfect backdrop for my morning meditation practice. Tweeting birds, the steady hum of passing cars, the pitter-patter of tiny feet—beauty is all around. And it's ready to support us!

5. Soothing sights, sounds, and smells. Meditation isn't just an energetic practice. Lovingly paying attention to the physical senses will serve you well. Try lighting candles to gaze at if you don't like closing your eyes during your practice. If the noises in your environment are too distracting, stream sounds of nature or gentle instrumental music. Burning incense, fragrant plants, and grasses or a nontoxic scented candle or diffusing essential oils can also create a calming effect in your space.

Think about how you can take each of these five suggestions and incorporate them into the perfect spot for your practice. Make a note of them here:

A place just for me: _____

_____

My favorite colors for peace and calm: _____

_____

Objects that make me smile: _____

_____

Elements from nature:_____

_____

My favorite sights, sounds, and smells:_____

_____

At the end of each phase (there are five in all), I'm going to lead you through a meditation that will help you process and seal in the lessons you just learned. Don't worry if you've never meditated before. You'll be guided step-by-step through each meditation.

Your first meditation is prefaced with a "Preparation for Your Meditation" section in which I'll tell you exactly how to get ready for your new practice. You'll also get instructions on how to position yourself during meditation and how to use my favorite breathing techniques to focus better and go deeper. Don't worry if this is new to you—I got you covered!

Your meditations are offered in two parts: "Words for Your Practice," a short motivational/inspirational message, and "Your Mantra," a phrase to repeat to yourself during silent breath work and reflection. Just follow along with an open mind and a receptive heart. That's all that's required to receive the benefits of meditation—the apps, fancy pillows, and Nag Champa can come when they may. Now, get ready for your first meditation!

Meditation for Self-Love

PREPARATION FOR YOUR MEDITATION

You just spent some time taking the first steps toward creating a physical and energetic practice that will support you throughout our journey together and in your role as a mother. This meditation will help you connect to your intuition and cultivate perfect discernment when it comes to knowing what is and what isn't in your healthiest and best interest.

Prepare your physical space by making sure you can be free from disruptive outside distraction for at least 10 minutes. That might mean telling your family you're taking a time-out and retreating to a quiet place behind a closed door.

POSITION

With this book in hand, find your Easy (or Comfortable) Seat— *sukhasana* in Sanskrit. This is one of the simplest and most commonly practiced yoga poses:

1. Sit up nice and tall.
2. Imagine a straight line traveling from the crown of your head and down your spine, ending at your bottom.
3. Cross your legs ("crisscross applesauce" for the moms of little ones out there).
4. Rest your hands on your knees or thighs with your palms facing up or down.

Of course, if sitting cross-legged is uncomfortable, feel free to choose any position that works for you. You can meditate almost anywhere, in any position—on the floor, in bed, or in a chair. You might want to lean against a wall or pillow for support or lie down if your intention is to rest or go to sleep. If you choose to sit on the floor, I recommend sitting on a firm cushion or pillow (see the illustration of my buckwheat-filled lotus pillow below) to help properly align the spine and hips. A blanket folded until it's four to six inches high can also replace a pillow in a pinch. I use inexpensive Mexican blankets like the ones you find in a yoga studio. Meditation requires only a willingness to take some time for yourself and your breath. The rest is just sprinkles on the ice cream.

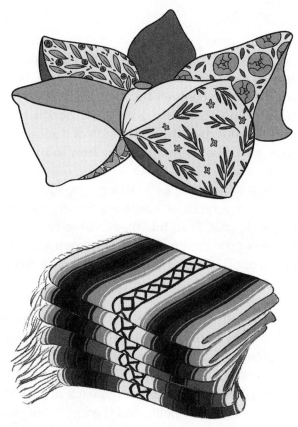

Once you're settled in your seat, take a big inhale and lift your shoulders up toward your ears. As you release your breath on your exhale, roll your shoulder blades back and down along your spine. You should find yourself sitting up even taller now, with broad shoulders and an open chest. Repeat this movement/ breath cycle a few times to really settle into your meditation posture, allowing yourself to release just a little more tension each time you exhale. You're going to revisit this position (or your own variation) for every meditation in this book, so make sure you feel comfortable and supported. If you become uncomfortable at any time during your meditation, shimmy and shift as necessary to settle into a better position. You're not a statue!

BREATH

Breathing is something you know how to do already, so I'm not going to complicate it here. However, I would like you to practice learning how to pay better attention to your breath. Focusing on your breath will help you quiet the mental chitchat (*chitta vritti* in Sanskrit) swirling around in your head. Breath work is one of the most basic but important elements of a good meditation practice. The good news is that learning how to tune in to your breath is easy.

In the spirit of keeping everything simple, I want you to focus on only three types of breathing for the meditations in this book: Easy Breath, Even Breath, and One-Two Breath. Note that only a few of the meditations in this book actually call for a specific kind of breath; on the others, use whichever one feels best in that moment.

1. Easy Breath: This technique is the breathing equivalent of Easy Seat. You've been breathing every day for your whole life, and all I'm going to ask you to do now is pay attention while you're doing it. Practice by simply following the path of your breath in through your nose, down the back of your throat, as it fills your lungs and your belly, and then as it exits your body through your nose or mouth. Allow your entire rib cage to expand and your belly to soften as you inhale. Allow yourself to settle even more comfortably into your seat with every exhale. Each breath cycle will end with you feeling more relaxed. There's no need to apply any extra effort while practicing Easy Breath. Just observing your breath will cause it to become smoother, longer, and deeper on its own.

2. Even Breath: If you have even the tiniest sense of rhythm, you can practice Even Breath with ease. Just match the length of each exhale to the inhale it followed. Focus on keeping your breaths smooth and relaxed. Silently counting during your inhales and exhales to make sure they match might be helpful to you at first. Pause for just a moment after each exhale, before beginning another breath cycle.

3. One-Two Breath: This is the most complicated breathing technique I'm offering to you, and it's complicated only because it requires a little math. But if you can multiply by two, you're all set. One-Two Breath is my go-to breathing technique when acute panic or anxiety strikes. It requires the most concentration, so it's perfect for moving my thoughts from fear to focus. It's easy. Inhale slowly, silently counting as your breath fills your body. Then, multiply that count by two and exhale for that length of time. For example, if you count to three during your inhale, your exhale should extend for a full six counts. Pause for moment at the bottom of each breath cycle.

GAZE

Closing your eyes isn't required, and if you don't feel safe or comfortable with your eyes closed during meditation, place your gaze softly upon an object such as a treasured belonging or a candle flame, or even on a particular spot in the room.

WORDS FOR YOUR PRACTICE

Now, before you divert your gaze from this page, I have some words to offer for your practice. I know how busy you are and that you don't need more unnecessary stuff floating around in your head, so each meditation in this book is set up to feel as easy as possible. Your meditations require only three simple actions:

1. Settling into your seat/posture
2. Reading a short motivational/inspirational message
3. Following your chosen breathing technique as you repeat a simple mantra in your head

From this point forward, you can choose your position and breathing technique, and I'll go right into your message and mantra. Pretty easy, right? Meditation works for me because it requires so little of my time and energy. It's perfect for my busy life, and that's why I love sharing it with other moms.

Read the following message slowly, taking time to pause after each sentence and breathe in the words. Imagine the words entering your body on your inhale and traveling to every part of you—from the crown of your head to the base of your seat, through your arms to your fingertips, and through your legs to your toes. Lean in to the spirit of the words and feel it filling your being with love, warmth, and good intentions.

> *Love is who you are and where you will return to every time you take just a few moments to say to yourself, "Yes, I see you, I love you, and you deserve my time and attention." Love is where you will return to every time you sit in stillness and allow your body, your mind, and your spirit to rest.*
>
> *Love is what will guide you when you ask, "Does this thought nourish my soul? Does this food nourish my body? Does this conversation nourish my intellect?" and so on. Love is what will guide you to always seek good feelings, safe spaces, and inspired interactions.*
>
> *Love is raising your standards, connecting to your innate wisdom, embracing your divinity, and accepting nothing less than what you know to be safe, healthy, and kind.*
>
> *Love is saying yes to feeling good. Loving yourself is calling everything that's love toward you and embracing it with a welcoming spirit.*

YOUR MANTRA

Begin breathing using whatever technique feels good to you in this moment. Read the following mantra silently or in a whisper. You'll repeat this mantra on every exhale for as long as you choose to sit in meditation. After reading your mantra, close your eyes or fix your gaze softly and drift easily into a state of peace and calm.

Love is who I am. I am worthy of being loved in every moment.

Phase 2

A SEED
IS PLANTED

CHAPTER 4

MAKING SPACE

When I was a teenager, I arranged the clothes in my closet according to their style—dresses, jackets, long-sleeved shirts, short-sleeved shirts, tank tops. In that order. The plastic hangers had to be of a particular width, and I used a pencil to make sure they were evenly spaced along the hanging rod. My cassette tape collection was always organized in alphabetical order by artist, and my books were arranged by the Dewey decimal system. Yes, for real. I considered junk drawers to be abominations, and I don't have one in my house today. I don't have obsessive-compulsive disorder. I recognize that OCD is a very real and sometimes debilitating mental-health condition, and that it is frequently used as a joke but is the farthest thing from it. But like many who do have the disorder, I used my regular organizing (and reorganizing) of my most treasured things as a way to manage my anxiety, as a coping mechanism to deal with what felt like overwhelming stress.

There are a lot of reasons—most rooted in my childhood—that I use organization to cope with anxiety even to this day. And I'm not ashamed to admit that messiness can still trigger an unhealthy response in me. I'm not sure if I'll ever get past needing things to be organized to feel safe and calm, and that's okay. Curing my anxiety has never been my goal. My method is to find a way to simply manage my response to stress and my expectations along with it.

If I made it my mission to cure my anxiety, I would only be adding another layer of stress that I just don't need. Have you ever been anxious about being anxious or worried that you might never stop worrying? Instead of judging myself for not being able to cure my anxiety, I accept it as just another part of my personality. At least for now, I'm a person whose anxiety is sometimes triggered by certain outside stressors, but that doesn't mean I don't still love myself or that I accept myself any less fully. Stress is an inevitable part of life, and if I want to live my life to the fullest, I had to learn to deal with it without creating more drama or self-judgment in the process.

There are times, however, when I've tried to ignore my triggers, thinking I'd moved past them or judging my response as unworthy of my time or attention. I get mad at myself for obsessing about something I've already dealt with, and I force myself to move on. That doesn't always lead to disaster, but it never turns out to be a good decision in the end. Instead, pretending environmental stress doesn't exist and invalidating my feelings about it almost always leads to prolonged and unnecessary low-grade suffering. Even I have to remind myself that I'm worth my time and attention. When I take the time to pay attention to my needs, I find comfort.

The shame of growing up poor and the connected shame about my childhood home have always been triggers for me, making me feel less than others and like an outsider. When I moved out on my own and was able to have total control of my living space—of how clean and organized it was—I thought I had fixed all the anxiety attached to growing up in a physically chaotic environment. And because I didn't give this issue of mine enough time and attention, it just kept festering until it inevitably came to the surface.

"Mess is the material from which life and creativity are built."
—Ralph Stacey

A Story about a Hideous F*cking Couch

I grew up poor. My family was angry and broken, our house was dirty and falling apart, and we kids were often neglected. We were never taken away from our parents, but threats were issued by school officials regularly. It was an ugly existence.

Now, miraculously and by the grace of God and my determination to be and do better, I have a beautiful home, healthy kids, and hope for the future. Don't get me wrong—it's not easy fighting the demons of a traumatic childhood every day. But a woman's gotta do what she's gotta do to get the life she wants.

I have five kids. They *wreck* stuff. I'm one of the cleanest and most organized people I know (because of, you know, poverty and my relentless dedication to managing my post-traumatic anxiety), but it's hard to guard a beige cotton canvas Pottery Barn slipcover against the assaults of five rowdy humans. It was washed so many times, the threads went bare and it started to rip at the seams.

This was a mental-health trigger like no other in my life. I looked at this couch and I saw the poor, dirty-kneed, messy little girl I was thirty years ago. I felt all the shame of being the child of a family people gossiped about and asked to "please move the bathtub out of your front yard because we have company coming."

It was just a beat-up family couch. You might have one, too. But for me, it was a symbol of a place I've escaped physically, but that remains very real in my psyche. I don't know if I'll ever fully escape the trauma of my childhood or the traces of shame that linger in its wake. All I know is how to confront it and make it smaller than who I know I am now—powerful, determined, gritty, fierce, vulnerable, and loving.

Something else is different today from back then. I'm surrounded by beautiful people who love me in all the right ways. When I told my friend how I was feeling about my ugly, effed-up couch, she didn't try to talk me out of my feelings. She validated them. Then, she sent me a link to a website that sells slipcovers nearly identical to Pottery Barn's at a steep discount. She understood that sometimes getting over something isn't about curing it. It's about dealing with it with honesty and action. We laughed about my hideous couch and all the other nonsense in our lives, and then we expressed gratitude for all the good. Life is messed up sometimes, but compassion always proves to be a good fix.

The happy ending to this story is that I impulse-bought a brand-new couch just a few weeks later, after I had some drama measuring Ugly Couch for the new slipcover (it felt like rocket science—which I discovered is almost as challenging as professional upholstering!). I also decided that washing slipcovers was something I'm no longer willing to do, which means, "No more food or markers in the living room, everrrr!!" bellowed in my best Faye-Dunaway-in-*Mommie-Dearest* voice. But it hadn't been until my small children started destroying my couch that I saw how ignoring a problem doesn't make it go away, and just as important, how toughing it out didn't make me any tougher.

We all have our personal triggers. Mine might resonate with you—or maybe it doesn't ring any bells at all. Your childhood could have been better or worse than mine. Maybe you see yourself in my story, or maybe you're thinking, "Get ahold of yourself, woman. It's just a couch." But what we all (most likely) share is that feeling of overwhelm. And without fail, physical and energetic clutter only make it worse, whether you acknowledge it or not. The couch was a painful reminder of the poverty and neglect I suffered growing up, and it took up a huge amount of physical space in a room I wanted to be a comfortable gathering spot for my family. Thinking about the couch—how to clean it, when to replace it, and how ridiculous it was that I was so profoundly triggered by it—was taking up far too much space in my head. Extreme negative events aren't the only cause of real injury. Tiny everyday stressors can do as much damage to your well-being as a single traumatic experience. Ugly Couch wasn't ruining my life, but it was creating low-grade suffering that I didn't need to endure any longer. So, it had to go.

Postscript: My youngest talks constantly about how much she misses the old couch. It's interesting how something that brought up so much pain for me represents comfort and happy memories for her. But my experiences are my own, not my children's, so I'm not going to make her hate Ugly Couch or feel shame about missing it. I'm not going to tell her how lucky she is to have nice things because I didn't. I am going to let her memorialize Ugly Couch as her favorite art canvas and snack spot. But yeah, I'd rather she keep missing it than we had kept it. New Couch was so necessary.

> *"My best teachers were mess, failure, death, mistakes, and the people I hated, including myself."*
> —Anne Lamott

I'm No Unicorn

If you've read this far, you know my message isn't about motherhood being all rainbows and sunshine. I'm no goddess, and I don't ride unicorns or bake pies from scratch. I'm just a woman trying to raise good people while maintaining some semblance of sanity and personal identity in the process. There are also a few big dreams I'd like to make happen, and I want to do good in the world. Maybe help some people. And *eat* pie while watching lots of Netflix.

I have a sense that you might be coming from the same place. You don't need to be worshipped, just appreciated. You don't want to be responsible for taking care of everything and everyone, but more often than not, you are. If you already have it all figured out, you can put down this book now—you're done! (But before you go, would you mind telling me the secret to getting to pee alone . . . with the door shut?)

The chaos of my childhood and most likely some hormonal/genetic factors have turned me into someone who longs for order and control. That's not so abnormal. But you can imagine that craving perfect order in a household of seven people and a constantly fluctuating number of pets can be problematic.

It has become my mission to find calm in the chaos, to access peace in the pandemonium. This second phase of the process is all about cleaning out, making space, and taking stock of everything awesome that you already have. You're going to work on tidying up your figurative closets in the next chapter, which can be a lot messier than actual closets. Let's start with the easy-*ish* part.

How Do You Want to *Feel?*

In Phase 1, you started preparing your fertile ground with foundational work to support your physical and energetic body and enhance your overall well-being. As I've realized in my years of gardening, a successful harvest starts with good soil. Your happiness in motherhood and beyond starts with a healthy body, mind, and spirit. But that body, mind, and spirit need to live somewhere, and it ought to be somewhere that makes you want to flourish. That's why the next step is all about creating a physical space for yourself and your family to grow and thrive in—one that feels spacious and looks beautiful.

Your home is wherever your heart is, so it should serve as an intimate physical container for what you love most. As you might have imagined, my childhood made this concept a bit tricky for me, so I understand that it might be tricky for you, too. Not everyone associates home with beauty, warmth, love, or safety. I get it. If you have mixed emotions about the concept of a happy home, let me share a few things that have worked for me.

My friend Elizabeth DiAlto, a women's leadership coach and stand-up comedian, gives a really beautiful instruction that leads her students to connect with their goals, dreams, and desires by utilizing their feelings, rather than their intellect. I'm going to revisit her method in greater depth in later lessons because it's helped me so much in my own practice, but for now, I want you to benefit from one of her lessons by thinking about how you want to *feel* when you're in your home. Coming from poverty, I get tripped up on creating beautiful spaces. I don't always feel confident when it comes to design. My experience with having "nice" things is pretty limited. Bringing the focus back to feelings helps so much. When I ask myself how a color, pattern, or object makes me feel, I forget all about whether it's stylish or appropriate.

It took me a while to get over being judgmental and get to the place of making this practice work for me, and the process was bumpy. Whenever my mother would go shopping for new clothes, she would either drag me along with her or subject me to an agonizingly painful one-woman fashion show when she got home. Second only to having her grandchildren closer, scoring a new shopping buddy was her greatest motivation to help me move back to New Jersey. "I don't know. Do I like this?" That question would drive me out of my mind! How could she not know what *she* likes? "Mom, are you seriously asking me to tell you what *you* like? What made you pick it out in the first place? What if nobody else's opinion mattered? Because it doesn't!" was always my response, and though I was an adult woman, I delivered it like a teenage mean girl.

Obviously, my mother struggled with insecurities about her physical appearance and sense of style, and I failed to treat her with compassion. And it was hypocritical, considering my struggles with second-guessing my own choices in regard to taste and style. I was being a not-so-awesome daughter, which wasn't cool. But on top of that, my attitude wasn't helping me fix what I didn't like about my own situation. I wanted to love my home. It's something I've craved since childhood.

The most effective tool I've used and continue to use to create a nourishing physical space is meditation. The particular meditation I use for this practice is inspired by one of my first experiences getting hypnotized by Grace Smith, author of *Close Your Eyes, Get Free*. In our session, she prompted me to go to my favorite place, a spot where I always feel happy and safe, and I was surprised by what surfaced. I remember thinking, "Take me to a secluded tropical beach, far away from *everything*." But instead, I found myself on the couch (before it turned into Ugly Couch) in my living room.

I was tucked snugly under a warm blanket into my favorite corner of the couch. The fireplace was glowing with red, orange, and white flames, and I could hear the crackling and popping of the fresh logs. It was Christmas morning, and the kids had just finished opening their presents. Brightly colored wrapping paper, torn and crumpled, littered the floor and crunched underfoot. The scent of our Christmas tree—packed with ornaments from past Christmases, including handmade ones from all the kids—filled the air. I was sipping a hot cup of apple cider, enjoying the scene, taking it all in. This is where my heart took me to when I was told to go to my happy place. And it's the scene I return to in meditation to connect to my heart's desire and to help me choose the elements and objects I want to bring into my perfect space. Meditating about my favorite place—my living room on Christmas morning—reminds me of how I want all my spaces to feel: warm and cozy, colorful and magical, filled with reminders of my family.

Now, close your eyes just for a moment and try to imagine your own favorite place. Think about all the details that make you love it so much. Really sink in and imagine yourself there. Be in the feeling your place inspires in you, and remind yourself of how easy it is to call in that feeling. I do this so often that I move easily into a relaxed state of peace and calm within seconds. You're going to be guided deeper into this in the next section.

Room to Grow

When I talk about a space being uncluttered, I don't mean perfectly clean and tidy. The dictionary defines clutter as "a disorderly heap or assemblage." A stranger could take one look at my work desk, covered with 1980s toys and unicorn coin banks, and easily describe it as cluttered. But my anxiety demands that I live in an *uncluttered* space. Uncluttered, for me, means "free from what is unnecessary." Clutter doesn't mean a lot of stuff—I have stuff everywhere. There are stacks of books all over my house that I don't have enough years left on this planet to read, and my beloved collections of elf statuettes and mythical creature tchotchkes (from the Yiddish word for knickknacks) are on display wherever I can fit them. Just looking at them brings me back to my favorite place.

My ceramic elves deliver just the right bit of whimsy and magic. The warm glow of my Himalayan salt lamps mimic the warmth of my crackling Christmas fire. And the handmade art and objects, created by friends and family alike, remind me of the handmade ornaments that every year adorn our tree. On rainy days or when I'm feeling blue or uninspired, I burn holiday-theme scented candles to conjure fuzzy feelings (I'm burning a pumpkin-scented candle as I write this). I fill my spaces with things that inspire me, and even though I have a lot of stuff, I never feel overwhelmed by it. It all supports my happiness.

A few years back, I bought a very popular book about tidying up with full expectations that it would change my life. It definitely delivered on that promise. I wasn't halfway through the book by the time the full contents of every closet, shelf, drawer, and miscellaneous storage container had been dumped, pored over, and (mostly) discarded. I launched myself into a cleaning, organizing, and purging frenzy that wore me out and scared my family a little. Like a cross between Martha Stewart and Godzilla, I would bellow, "This doesn't spark joy! TOSS IT!"

None of this was the book's fault. My husband put an end to the madness before I could finish reading it. The main issue was that I wasn't giving myself time to sit with the decisions—it was all slash-and-burn. I was only considering how I was feeling in the moment, with no grand vision or pause to feel into the process. I was focused on making things smaller and tidier rather than expansive and soul pleasing.

It shouldn't have been about tossing everything out in a crazed frenzy. It should have been about discerning what I wanted my space to look like and taking the time to create that space. "Discernment" is one of my favorite words because it feels wise and intentional. A discerning woman doesn't rush to judgment. She's thoughtful and self-aware.

Even if you're already in love with your home, you might find the following practice useful in creating a space that's even more emotionally nourishing, that's even more an expression of you, one that supports your interests and passions. It's also a great practice to share with your children as they develop an interest in designing their own spaces. It teaches them how to be intentional about what they bring in, and also what they let go. I call this process of checking in with your feelings before making a judgment Divine Discernment (and I'm going to return to it a lot in this book).

DIVINE DISCERNMENT (FOR CREATING NOURISHING SPACES) 101

It's not hard to practice Divine Discernment. It's really just another way to "check yourself before you wreck yourself"—one of my favorite mantras (and bits of hip-hop wisdom). Here's how to build your practice of Divine Discernment in three steps.

Step 1: Meditate. Set aside 10 to 15 minutes of quiet time when you can be left undistracted. Revisit the prompt I gave you earlier in this chapter by closing your eyes and calling in the sights, sounds, and smells of your favorite place. Notice every detail about the environment. Everything is significant. Notice how you feel in your body as you settle into your visualization. Remain there for just a few minutes or for as long as it feels good. You'll notice that this activity is similar to the one for creating your perfect meditation space. You're building on that here, going deeper.

Step 2: Journal. Open your eyes and write down everything you remember. Make sure you're writing this in a place you can access again easily, like a notes app in your phone or a journal. Write as much as possible, describing your favorite place in great detail. What you write will guide you in identifying the elements in your environment that do and do not currently serve you, and will help you figure out what to add and what not to add in the future. It acts as a bubble of protection against impulse buying when you're walking down the clearance aisles (which happen to be my own personal kryptonite).

Step 3: Integrate. Put the first two steps of this practice to the test by walking into any room in your house, picking up a random item, and asking yourself, "How does this align with my vision of my perfect space?" If it doesn't, ask yourself if it's something you really need or that has to be put on display. Does it have a real purpose? Is it necessary, or does it feel like clutter? Start in the space where you spend the most time or where you desire the biggest shift in energy. Your bedroom might fit this description. *Where* you start doesn't matter as much as just getting started. Soon, you'll be using this technique in every area of your life, physical and energetic.

Important Caveat: This practice should not be carried out in your partner's or child's spaces, at least not by you. I know that none of the 28,373 miniature rubber cartoon animal figurines living in your kid's closet serve the grand vision of your safe and happy place, but you might have to tolerate them for a bit longer. Remember, though, you can share this practice with your loved ones and let them lead the way in making their own divinely influenced decisions. Nobody wants Godzilla invading their space and stomping all over their stuff. RIP, my husband's power biscuit joiner (whatever that was).

For more practical, easy, and soulful solutions for organizing every space in your home, including your bedroom closet, kitchen, and even your medicine cabinet, download my 21-Day Soul Cleanse for free by registering for your book bonuses at BexLife .com/book.

And even if you're not able to cleanse every room or complete every activity or suggestion in this book, know that once we begin to shift our perspective on something, action inevitably follows. We can't help but look around at our space and begin to see where we might shift it. Divine Discernment begins with observation, so if all you can do right now is observe, you've begun the most important part of the work!

CHAPTER 5

CLEARING
THE WEEDS

There's something about a good quote that makes me feel like it was written just for me. It speaks right to the heart of whatever matter I'm stressing over and puts me at ease, at least for a little while—enough time to take a breath, hit the pause button on the worry that's playing over and over in my head, and collect myself before moving on with my day. Reading a motivational quote can feel like a mini-meditation, my favorite kind.

Throughout this book, I've included some of my favorite quotes. I used the quotes in this chapter to support what you're about to learn because I find that nothing clears the weeds quicker than someone else's wisdom. Most of the quotes are attributed to the person who *probably* said them (but not necessarily the first person to), and one is listed without attribution (because the Internet is a den of thievery and lazy research and I couldn't find a reliable source despite my best efforts). I do know that the Buddha, probably the most misquoted person who has ever lived, is responsible for none of these.

But no matter the source, when we are able to ground ourselves in wisdom's soil, we can have a clearer perspective on what is right and important. And through others' experiences, we are better able to understand, negotiate, and, ultimately, let go of our own. Sure, we can break our backs out in the field, yanking out each weed by its root, or we can enlist friends, fellowships, books, teachers, and other resources to join us in the garden.

And sometimes, we just need a guide to show us how to get there faster.

Life is filled with weeds—and some of them are so beautiful, we're willing to let them stay. But some of them only strangle new growth. Throughout this chapter, we'll begin to see which parts of our life story are worth hanging on to, and what parts we can finally begin to surrender to make room for more.

Working with What We Have

"Accept what is, let go of what was, and have faith in what will be."
— Sonia Ricotti

Acceptance is something I talk about a lot. It's become a theme in every area of my life because it supports ease, something I look for in each moment, especially as a person managing anxiety and the trials of motherhood on a daily basis. Acceptance means different things to different people. For me, it's not about tolerating the intolerable. I don't accept things like bigotry, injustice, or meanness. There are some things that are simply not okay. But at the same time, I know even the tough stuff is part of the deal. Acceptance is about observing life like we do the seasons. I can't control the snowstorm, but I can shovel the drive. We should acknowledge what is, understand our responsibility in each situation, and allow for an outcome that is partly out of our control and partly within our power to change. The truth is, sometimes it *is* my circus and the monkeys are all mine. Other times, it may or may not be my show, and I'm only willing to claim a couple of the actors. Motherhood is a constant practice of sorting out if it was my monkey who flung the poop and if it's my job to clean it up (always quietly hoping that someone else will show up to do it for me).

Mothers do not hatch from eggs fully formed and complete with a catalog of wisdom and cupcake-decorating skills. I've been at this gig for 21 years, and I still call on my friends and qualified professionals to make my kids' birthday cakes. We have to learn as we go, and we have to *un*learn at the same time. We were people before we became mothers. Motherhood is no different from any other role in that we bring baggage into it—preconceived ideas about the experience and ourselves, old stories, and well-formed habits and ways of being. When the experience doesn't match up to our expectations or challenges our old ideas, we can find ourselves in resistance, the opposite of acceptance and allowing. The resistance creates tension, and the monkey poop hits the fan.

Let's revisit motherhood as a garden. Imagine weeds as the stories and old habits from your past that have kept you from feeling fully confident in your mothering abilities or in just loving yourself as a woman separate from your role as a mother. Without getting into whether or not a weed is actually a bad thing or how "weeds are flowers too, once you get to know them" (thank you, Winnie-the-Pooh), let's just agree that weeds can and will mess with your garden goals if left unattended. They take up space, hoard nutrients, and suffocate new growth. There are times when weeds *can* be a welcome addition to a landscape, but for the sake of our current work, weeds can kick rocks.

Releasing Old Stories

> *"You are the sky. Everything else is just the weather."*
> — Pema Chödrön

Here's the thing about old stories and habits: they are not you. Just like the weather is not the sky; it comes and goes. And the weeds are not the garden—they can be plucked and discarded. You are a whole, complex, dynamic being who can't be defined by any one experience or role. Nevertheless, you might sometimes believe that you are. You might be holding on to an old story about an experience that happened a long time ago and feel like you can never be what you want to be because you were once a person who did "bad" things—or, more often than not, who had "bad" things done to them. Trauma doesn't disappear overnight, and a professional may be required to help us heal. But that healing begins when we realize that the old stories don't serve us, no matter how they might have defined our experience.

I used to suffer from terrible anxiety, and I took it out on my children. Their messy rooms were a constant source of stress for me. Instead of accepting that they were little kids who needed help keeping their things organized, my anxiety would be triggered and I would lose my patience, yelling and threatening to throw out their precious belongings. One time—a particularly ugly time—I flung my oldest daughter's clarinet down the steps after finding it on her bedroom floor. She was only nine years old at the time. I was in the middle of a contentious divorce from her father, and I had lost control of the situation and myself. So, I took all my pain out on her. It was cruel of me to act that way, and now, even all these years later, I still hold guilt about my behavior. That entire period of my life was a dark and stormy time that has since passed. It was just the weather, not the wholeness of who I was or the potential of who I would become. The guilt and shame I still feel about it are my weeds. They take up space in my heart, crowding out the flowers—the good stuff I'd like to cultivate—and preventing me from growing fully into the mother I want to be. It's my work to pull those weeds whenever they pop up.

Your weeds might be the little doubts that keep creeping into your day, getting in the way of feeling good. Don't dismiss them as nothing. Your happiness is important, and even the tiny, seemingly trivial things that get in its way need your attention. Notice those thoughts and feelings, and forgive yourself for having them. Remind yourself that you're more than them and move on.

It would be easy for me to say, "I am who I am, and there's nothing I can do to change," but it wouldn't feel very good. It wouldn't make me a better person, partner, friend, or mother. I want to experience ease in my life, but I know that it takes some work to get to that place of ease. Like the acorn, I accept that I have to crack open to grow. You probably feel the same way, or you wouldn't be reading this book. You want to be a better woman/mother/*everything*, but you know you have some work to do. Congratulations, that is an extremely healthy outlook! Accepting that you're a little messed up is a good thing. It's way better than freaking out every time you spot a weed, or notice your perfectly pretty petals starting to brown around the edges. A healthy garden is one that is maintained regularly. You gotta pluck the weeds, trim the parts of the plants that are no longer thriving, and feed and water what you want to grow. So, let's get to it—together.

Purging Negative Thoughts

> *"Never be a prisoner of your past. It was just a lesson, not a life sentence."*
> — Unknown

In Chapter 1, we discussed the simple three-step practice of letting go of negative thoughts. That exercise has given me so much freedom, so much emotional space, to create new thoughts and more nourishing self-care practices. Writing down negative thoughts puts them in a place outside of my head. Talking back to them with the truth injects perspective and wisdom into the conversation. My life coach refers to it as a daily purge. I sometimes call it "taking an energetic dump," which is far less elegant but gets the point across. I remove the energetic toxicity so new, more positive energy can fill the space.

This practice helps with identifying the everyday nuisance weeds that pop up on a regular basis. As soon as they start pushing through to the surface, I see them and pluck them out. They're tiny and weak, so it's easy. "I can't believe I forgot to send in the permission slip for the school trip *again*. Her teacher must think I'm a terrible mother." I'm a busy mom. Everyone gets that. *Pluck! Toss!* Moving on. However, old stories have deeper roots. You can think you've dealt with them for good only to find them popping up again and again. A current conflict with my oldest son works like a pickaxe, hacking away at my ground and exposing all the pain I've yet to address from issues that would be easier to keep buried. Old stories about my relationship with my parents, ways they hurt me, and how that damage shaped me as a mother still haunt me today. And when those roots are exposed, deeper work is necessary. Don't worry—we're going to do that deeper work together, too.

Getting rid of these persistent weeds doesn't have to be a hopeless endeavor, and maintaining a healthy garden doesn't have to consume every moment of your existence. I know all too well what it feels like to be a prisoner of the past and how to go through the process of overcoming it. Reminding myself that my stories are separate from who I am helps soothe the sting of regret. Using tools to sort the weeds from the flowers and nourish what I want to grow helps me move forward with confidence. Clearing old, deeply rooted weeds can be a big job at first, but it's well worth the effort. And the process *will* get easier—it's just going to take time, patience, and some deep digging to get it done.

Putting Down Unnecessary Burdens

"Sometimes you have to put something down to lift something up."
— Anna Gannon

Anna Gannon is a meditation teacher and writer, and my friend. She delivers truths about motherhood that both tug at the heartstrings and teach valuable lessons about what it means to be a mama in this modern world. Her Instagram account is one I follow for inspiration and to remind me that I am not alone. None of us are. This is a story about Anna's daughter, Annabell, that she shared with an image of the quote above:

> Being the toddler that she is, this weekend, Annabell had her hands full of toys while simultaneously attempting to pick more up. As I watched her struggling to fit them all in her tiny arms, the mother in me said, 'Annabell, sometimes you have to put something down to lift something up.' When the words left my mouth, I thought about how hard a lesson this is for so many of us to learn. How much time we spend trying to gather everything in our lives, leaving little space for us to lift up something else. It's amazing how much observing a toddler can teach you about us as adults.

I was already in the process of writing this book, so I made a note of Anna's post immediately because it captured my message better than I ever could (a benefit of having smart friends). We have to identify and let go of what's unnecessarily burdening us in order to make space for what we want and need. I'm reminded of another one of my favorite quotes: "I wonder how much of what weighs me down is not mine to carry." This chapter is about noticing and weeding out old negative stories, those unnecessary energetic burdens, and allowing yourself to put down what isn't yours to carry (or what *is* yours that can finally be let go). But how do you do that?

For the past couple of years, I've offered a 21-day journal-ing challenge to my audience. Each day builds on the previous one and asks the participant to dig a little deeper, uncovering a little more about themselves. I'm going to let you skip ahead to Days 18 to 20, when it's time to write "The Story of You." (Visit BexLife.com/journal for a free download of the full 21–day journal.) Your story will be broken up into three parts: from conception or birth (whichever holds more significance for you) to 18 years old, from age 18 to the present day, and a positive prediction of your future.

The purpose of this activity is to place you in the role of an objective observer, a biographer. I understand that it can be a big, emotional undertaking to examine your whole life at once, but I encourage you to approach this activity as dispassionately as possible. If you can fool yourself into thinking you're merely a biographer, a person tasked with telling the facts of anoth-er's life, you aren't attached to what was or what will be. You hold no judgment or prejudice. If it's easier for you to create a bullet-point timeline instead of writing it out like a long nar-rative, then do that. Write in the third-person voice (talking about yourself as another would). Like everything else in this book, do what you can, when you can, using the time and the resources available. Here's a short example from my personal practice. I wrote it when I first started "weeding" through my old mental stories.

> I was born in 1978 in a small town 10 miles south of Trenton, NJ. The town was built around the Roebling Steel Co. mill (which closed shortly before I was born), and my family lived in the historic village section. I have two sisters, one 10 years older and the other 3 years younger.
>
> I never knew my biological father. My mother cheated on her husband (the man who would raise me and be the one I would call my father) a lot, and I was the product of one of her affairs. And because the person she was having an affair with at the time of my conception was Black, and that would become obvious at my birth, she had to confess.

A series of very questionable decisions followed. My mother and father attempted to hide the pregnancy and planned to give me up for adoption and tell everyone who knew about me that I had died in childbirth. But at the last minute, my father received what he interpreted as a divine message and changed his mind. So, they kept me and hid the identity of my biological father, but I always new my dad wasn't related to me by blood. My mother offered some more details to me when I was 32, but I wouldn't confirm the name and identity of my biological father until I was 36 years old and reading the emailed results of a DNA test while attending to my mother on her deathbed.

Heavy stuff, I know. It wasn't easy to write it then, and it isn't easy to share it now. But this is a part of my story that I've struggled with since, well, birth. It has shaped a lot of who I am today, and it needed to be uprooted and examined. Your story might be more or less dramatic than what you just read. That doesn't matter. What's important is that you get all the most significant memories and events written down. I keep my story in a document that I can add to. The work is ongoing, so the document will never really be finished. Going back to it, seeing what I wrote, and examining my evolving feelings about it all have been healing for me. Knowing that I can leave the words in the document and that I don't have to carry them around with me allows for a lightness of being that I didn't enjoy earlier in life (but wish I could have).

Let's get you started on writing your story. Remember to take your time.

THE STORY OF YOU

Step 1: Start at the beginning. In third-person voice, in story format, or in a bullet-point timeline, write about your childhood from birth or conception to age 18 (or the age when you began to consider yourself an adult). I know I could write a whole book about any one aspect of my life (you're kind of reading it now), but don't feel like you have to turn any part of this activity into a novel. You can always add to your work later.

Step 2: Tackle the adult years. Oh, all the adulting you've done—leaving the nest, getting your name on your very own utility bills, and starting a family! Wheeeee! You've done and experienced a LOT. Write it down. Make sure it's true. Just the facts. If anything you write brings up an emotional response, just let it happen and move on. We'll deal with that in a bit.

Step 3: It's time for your positive predictions. This is probably the most challenging step of the whole activity because it's calling upon you to flex your imagination muscle. It's the part where you get to fantasize a bit, and that might feel self-indulgent or unfamiliar. Let yourself lean in to this step. Take your time and have fun with it. Describe in detail the future manifestation of your present-day hopes and dreams—all aspects of your life, working out just like you planned.

Step 4: Grab your highlighter. Once you've finished Steps 1, 2, and 3 with satisfaction (knowing you can always go back and add more later), you can start the review process. This will help you sort out the weeds that need some attention. Grab a highlighter (or use the highlighter tool on your device if you are doing this activity electronically), go back to the beginning of your document, and highlight any part that elicits a negative emotional response in you—anything that triggers you, that makes you squirm, or that you wouldn't feel comfortable sharing publicly or even with friends or family. These are the deep-rooted weeds. These are the stories that you might not think about consciously, but that hide out in your subconscious. Identifying these pesky little parts of your past, the stuff that can hold you back and weigh heavily on your energetic body (your mind, heart, and spirit), is enough for now. You're just highlighting them today. You'll use this work again for future exercises in later chapters.

"I do some of my best thinking while pulling weeds."
— Martha Smith

Just by uncovering a few old stories that have been buried deep, you can begin the healing process of letting them go. You don't have to do anything to start feeling relief. Finally bringing your negative stories into the light of day allows you to feel a little less burdened by them. You can start to observe the triggering parts of your story as things that are separate from you. The fact that they're no longer happening, that they live in the past, is proof that they're merely energetic things that you have the permission and power to leave behind. They might still hurt—that's real. I'm not dismissing your feelings. Just know that soon, they'll start to hurt less.

In one of my favorite movies, *Labyrinth*, the young hero, Sarah, proclaims to the Goblin King, Jareth (played by the spectacularly strange and beautiful David Bowie), "You have no power over me!" You are now Sarah. Tell those old stories that they have no power over you. And then watch—*poof!*—as your stories shatter into a million pieces. Okay, so maybe it won't happen just like in the movies (does it ever?). It will probably take more than one go-round to unload a lifetime of negative self-talk. But know that it is possible to release the grip of your negative stories, maybe even just a *little* bit, right now. It doesn't have to feel hard, and it doesn't have to take forever.

We'll revisit and build upon this activity later. For now, feel good about the work you've done so far. You've unloaded some serious energetic weight that you've been dragging around for a while. You'll start to notice how understanding where some of your worries and unproductive habits come from allows you to not get so discouraged when they start to crop up again. There were times when recalling painful memories would send me into a panic attack that would land me in the emergency room. Now, I can not only deal with my memories rationally, but I grow every time I do. That's a big reversal, I know. I also know that you can do it, too. You won't fall down the rabbit hole of anxiety because you'll recognize that your head is just trying to tell you an old story, one that is no longer your reality. You'll feel lighter, and that will affect how you relate to everyone around you as you show up as a better friend, partner, and mother. And this is only the beginning of your transformation!

CHAPTER 6

REAP WHAT YOU'VE ALREADY SOWN

This chapter is the one I most looked forward to writing. Because I'm awesome at gratitude! I am genuinely excited about every single thing life has to offer (annoying, I know). But that excitement doesn't come naturally. I have learned over the years to cultivate gratitude into such a powerful force that it overwhelms a lot of the negative voices that would like me to think, be, and do otherwise. Every day, I repeat a silent "thank you" in my head 100 times, working to recognize that every breath is a gift. Because it is quite literally my job to teach other people how to find joy in every moment!

And yet, despite all this experience and excitement, when I sat down to write about gratitude, I drew a total blank. I struggled to find the right words, with how to talk about it in an authentic way. Because the truth is that there is a lot in my life right now that makes gratitude hard. No matter what is going on in my day, or how happy I feel, there is a shadow to my joy ever since my son moved away.

I have so much to be grateful for, but there are forces at work and unavoidable realities that have changed my gratitude practice and the way I experience joy. With greater awareness comes, well, greater awareness. And as I move through the world and expand my perspective, I see how my practice must expand with it. In a way, though, gratitude is all about giving thanks in the middle of our toughest struggles. So, I persist in my practice. Just as I mentioned in the introduction to this book, the work I've done and that I offer you has supported me through my hardest moments. To this day, it's the practice I turn to during my biggest trials.

Creating a truly healthy gratitude practice—one that leads you to connect to loving feelings about yourself, others, and your experiences—can be tricky for thinking, feeling people who are aware of the hurt that life has to offer or who have suffered a lot of it themselves.

Just moving through life as women (and I include all women here, regardless of which sex organs they were born with) is challenging. The nature of the world subjects us to a lot of unfairness and stress. Our bodies, how we express ourselves, and the choices we make for our families are all examined and discussed by people who too often have not invited us to have a say (and I'm not even talking about our immediate families, with all their old wives' tales and unsolicited opinions). Consider how deeply personal issues—such as how we get pregnant, give birth, or decide to feed our babies—are hotly debated on public forums, with other people feeling like they know what's right for us better than we do. The work we do as mothers is constantly critiqued and managed by outside entities, and that intrusion influences how we feel about ourselves. Everyone from our Facebook "friends" to our elected officials to our mother-in-law has something to say about how we decide to live our lives. That can seriously mess with our heads *and* hearts.

Giving Ourselves What We Deserve

Why am I talking about the social and political pressures of motherhood in a chapter about gratitude? Because gratitude is linked to value. It's an expression of appreciation and love for what's good in our lives, the abundance we enjoy. Expressing gratitude for something is saying, "Thank you," while also acknowledging, "I deserve this." And that can feel super hard for a lot of mothers. At the same time that we're receiving messages of celebration about motherhood, we're usually being shown that we don't deserve much, even of what we need. We want to be grateful, so we teach ourselves to be grateful for crumbs, and that has huge consequences for our emotional health.

Like a lot of women, gratitude and I have a complicated relationship. On top of dealing with all the mixed messages that society has dumped on mothers, I've also had to deal with my parents' messed-up views about money and its influence on their sense of personal value. My parents struggled to make ends meet, and often didn't. From the time I was little, I was aware of the cost of everything, including basics like food and electricity. My parents' fears about money, combined with their interpretation of Christian teachings, manifested a lot of conflicting ideas that were then passed down to me.

I was taught that honest hard work was virtuous but having too much money was not. Rich people were bad (I wasn't sure why), but rich people were also the ones who donated clothes for my younger sister and me. Most of my childhood lessons about money—and by extension wealth, charity, value, and gratitude—left me feeling confused. "Work hard. Make money. But not too much! If you make more than you need, which is not a lot, give it away."

This made me feel like I didn't deserve much, and feeling like I didn't deserve much led me to give too much of myself away. So many of us have determined our value based on the opinions and ideals of other people. And if we don't measure up to those ideals, then why would we deserve anything nice, anyway? We already feel guilty about being out of the house too much for work, so we say no to the much-needed girls' night out. We feel like our kids never get alone time with us, so we don't make alone time for our partners. Have you ever felt like you were losing yourself in motherhood? That's what happens when you leave nothing of yourself *for* yourself. It's what happens when you don't value yourself and protect your energy.

Like I said, I still grapple with these issues. Intellectually, I know I have inherent value and that I have a lot to offer to the world. I know it's okay to enjoy nice things and find pleasure in the fruits of my labor. I've planted seeds, I've done the important work of taking care of myself and others, and I deserve to reap the good things I've sown. The same is true for you. You have value that deserves to be recognized and a spirit that deserves nurturing. How can a gratitude practice help with all of this? That's what I want to share.

The way I was viewing gratitude didn't take into account that many women have trouble feeling grateful for anything in their lives. You can't force yourself to find things to be happy about, and the more you try to force the process, frequently, the less grateful you feel. That's why when people mention starving children, we don't feel any better. We just feel worse that there are starving children. There's no value in faking your way to happiness or taking on a Pollyannaish attitude. As mothers, we have enough to do. Everyday stress is more than enough to turn sitting down and thinking happy thoughts into just another chore on your list. And when you add outside pressures and criticisms, inherited negative thought processes, and internalized feelings of unworthiness (oh my!), it's easy to feel like you have nothing left to give.

I want to share how I accessed feelings of gratitude even while experiencing my own difficult circumstances, and how that was actually the most important time to lean on my practice. I also want to show how *easy* it is to create an effective practice. My gratitude practice, which is really an evolving *set* of practices, has given me so much. I know it can do the same for other women just like me.

I have learned that having a consistent gratitude practice is one of the best and easiest ways to achieve that magical, mythical unicorn that you've definitely heard about, the one you're probably craving and everyone is always asking me about. It's called *balance*, and it's what everyone wants but no one seems to be able to achieve. Let's take a great big inhale and say it on the exhale: "Balance." Want some? Let's get it!

There are so many ways to practice gratitude. Perhaps you already have a way to say thank you every day. Saying thank you isn't really the hard part. However, I noticed that it was easy to be lazy in my practice, to phone it in instead of showing up. For instance, I set aside time to list all the things I was grateful for, but it was rushed and superficial—"I'm grateful for my family, my house, and food in the refrigerator." Of course, none of those things are trivial, but my effort was lazy. Because I didn't take the time to sit in gratitude and allow myself to *feel* grateful, I didn't experience balance in those moments. I had to come up with practices that are mindful—that make gratitude a weighty and powerful counter to whatever is stressing me out.

It's a Beautiful Glass

There's a movie called *Human* by Yann Arthus-Bertrand that features a friend of mine, John Halcyon Styn, a master storyteller and "gifting evangelist." I was first introduced to John through a viral clip of him sharing a story about his grandfather, Caleb. John's story—one about love, loss, family, perspective, and gratitude—captured my heart immediately. It struck me so powerfully that it made me pause and consider how I might do better in practicing gratitude and, more important, how I judged every moment of my life. I felt compelled to reach out to tell John how much his story affected me, and we've collaborated a few times since then. Each time was a gift. I count John among my many blessings.

The story went something like this:

John's grandparents had been married for 65 years, and his grandmother had become his grandfather's caretaker in many ways, including as his driver. Shortly after her death, John, concerned about his grandfather, went for a visit.

When John asked Grandpa Caleb how he was doing, he joyfully answered with a story about how he had discovered that he could go all over the city with a $4 bus pass. He told John that the bus got him to the grocery store, where he met an employee who he asked to help him with his grocery list because his wife "had recently changed her residence to Heaven." John found his positivity remarkable. He smiled and said, "Grandpa, you always help me see the glass as half full." To which Grandpa Caleb replied, "It's a beautiful glass."

Can you feel that? Hearing those four simple words created a seismic shift in my perspective on gratitude. The half-empty/half-full glass metaphor is one we're all familiar with. You might even have heard a slightly different riff on the theme: "The glass isn't half empty or half full. The glass is refillable." That was a favorite of mine for a long time, but I had to let it go, along with the idea that the key to happiness was always looking on the bright side. Bad stuff happens and denying that fact doesn't make it go away. And the idea of having to "refill" my glass with happy stuff all the time felt exhausting. I just wanted a way to enjoy life, to appreciate what's good, and to not get so hung up on what isn't working. Looking at the glass—the metaphor for my life, the big picture, and what was true and real—as beautiful was just the message I needed to hear.

You see, what's in the glass doesn't matter. It can be great one day, awful the next, or just show up as a mix of good and bad (as is true on *most* days). But it doesn't change the constant and prevailing truths of our experience. The glass—the truth of who we are—never changes. And that glass is beautiful.

Managing the motherload is about creating balance, but balance doesn't mean equal parts of everything. I can't tell you how often I've been asked how I manage to achieve work–life balance, and every time I just want to scream, "There's no such thing!" Because that kind of balance doesn't really exist. I don't end my workday by tying up everything I had to do with a pretty little bow and then doing the same thing after spending time with my family, but I do end each day feeling a sense of balance. Some days feel amazing, and gratitude is easy. Other days are messy and feel like a dumpster fire. I had to redefine gratitude for myself.

> *"Learn to get in touch with the silence within yourself and know that everything in life has purpose. There are no mistakes, no coincidences, all events are blessings given to us to learn from."*
> — Elisabeth Kübler-Ross

I'm going to give you three different gratitude practices that you can use individually, mix and match, or stack together to make it personal to you. These are also appropriate to share with your family, so I encourage you to bring your kids into the mix. Expressing gratitude should feel like a celebration, a harvest of what's good. It should be fun!

A One-Word Gratitude Practice for Balance

Motherhood is hard some days. It beats me up. *And* I'm a mother of five gorgeous, brilliant humans who bring me a lot of joy (especially when they're sleeping—they're *so* cute when they're sleeping). As I've discussed, I deal with a lot of emotional messiness passed down from my parents. *And* I have the tools to manage it. Lately, it feels like the world is collapsing in on itself, and it doesn't help that the news basically plays like a collection of scenes from a post-apocalyptic dystopian fantasy (where is Katniss when you need her!?). *And* I'm surrounded by smart, compassionate friends who are doing amazing work in the world and inspire me to do better every day. These "and" statements are how I create a sense of balance in my life and separate the contents of the glass from the glass itself. They're also one of my favorite ways to express gratitude.

My "and" statements are a reminder that I'm here, I'm safe, and in every moment I can choose peace over panic. Oftentimes, when I'm in the middle of panic, emotional pain, or intense worry, it feels like that's all there is. I forget all about the "and." Instead, I get stuck in the "or." I can feel pain *or* pleasure. I'm sad *or* I'm happy. I'm panicking *or* I'm calm. But the truth is that life is never all bad. This is when I call on the "and." The "and" is magic. The "and" gives me hope because it shows me the truth of every "bad" situation.

"My bills are stacking up, *and* I have a warm bed to sleep in tonight."

"I sabotaged my healthy eating with all that junk last night, *and* I can choose my next meal with love."

"Everyone is putting all their problems on me, *and* I have the power to set stronger boundaries."

You're going to ask, add, and affirm by coming up with your own "and" statements and then adding a simple mantra to create a personal one-line affirmation. It is through this practice of gratitude that we begin to realize balance based on one word—the all-powerful, magical "and."

Step 1: Ask. Sit quietly for a few moments and ask yourself, "What is causing me discomfort right now?" I use the word "discomfort" to describe all levels of stress on the spectrum, from real pain to everyday annoyances. Write whatever comes to mind in a short list of 3 to 10 items, max.

Step 2: Add. Based on my examples above, write a statement to add to each of your answers from Step 1 that is also true but feels positive and empowering. Example: "I feel completely overwhelmed by everything on my to-do list, *and* I have so many amazing things going on in my life that are keeping me busy and excited about my future."

Step 3: Affirm. Read each "and" statement out loud and repeat the following affirmation mantra after each one: "My glass is beautiful, and I'm grateful for all the things that fill it up."

This exercise has totally changed the way I approach complaining. It also gave me a way to teach my kids how to reframe their grievances (teenagers tend to have a LOT of those). As soon as a negative thought or "woe is me" moment creeps up, I create an "and" statement to create balance. I don't invalidate my feelings or those of my kids, and I don't tell myself or them that it's wrong to think so-called negative thoughts. The last thing I want to do is dismiss my kids' feelings or let them think they don't have a right to share what's upsetting them. Expressing frustration, anger, overwhelm—all the things that cause us discomfort—is an important part of taking care of our health. Having the ability to remind ourselves of what's good maintains balance. This practice provides my kids and me with a way of venting that serves our health and happiness, and it can do the same for you. All you have to remember to do is the three A's: *ask*, *add*, and *affirm*!

A Morning Practice for Gratitude and Service

Every morning, or at least on the mornings that begin *good* days, I practice the same ritual. As soon as I open my eyes, before I use the bathroom or say good morning to my husband, before my littlest one climbs into bed to cuddle my "mommy boobies," I say a three-part prayer that lists what I'm grateful for and inspires me for my day ahead.

Let me explain why I'm using prayer instead of meditation here. Some people say prayer is when you ask God (or whatever name you use to describe the collective consciousness or an entity greater than yourself) to listen, and meditation is when you listen to God. Most of the time, the terms are interchangeable when it comes to my personal practice. I believe that each one of us is a tiny piece of the collective consciousness. Through prayer and meditation, we are able to acknowledge this fact and plug more deeply into that mysterious energy force that fuels us all. In doing so, we can call on our inner God wisdom. This is because meditation is a listening activity, one where we call in the insights instead of offering them, so we sit quietly and just listen. In meditation, there's no attachment to anything that comes after. You don't have to *do* anything with the information you receive or the insights that pop up from within. Prayer feels more active to me. It has a specific purpose and calls for a desired result—not just peace and calm. I say a prayer every morning to recognize what's good in my life and activate me for spreading around the love and abundance.

Part 1: "Thank You, Thank You, Thank You." I picked up this part from one of my spiritual mentors, Dr. Wayne W. Dyer. He repeated this prayer every morning and even wrote it on pieces of notepaper that he posted next to his bed. It was part of his daily ritual and the way he often ended his prayers. Dr. Dyer wrote that before shaving each day, he would repeat, "Thank you, God, for this life, for my body, for my family and loved ones, for this day, and for the opportunity to be of service. Thank you, thank you, thank you." I love ritual and crave simplicity, so this was a perfect addition to my morning practice.

To really seal in the power of the words, I say them out loud in a whisper. Just like writing down a thought gives it life and helps you remember it better, saying your prayer out loud helps it resonate more deeply. Meister Eckhart, a German philosopher born in the thirteenth century (aka a really old smart dude), once said, "If the only prayer you ever say in your entire life is thank you, it will be enough." If you want to end your morning ritual right here, you're good to go! I suspect, however, that a day of momming might require a little more juice than that, so consider also trying out the next two parts of this ritual.

Part 2: Three Little Things. This part is easy. Just name three things you're grateful for right now. I like to challenge myself by listing things I've never listed before. A house, food in the pantry, a healthy body, my beautiful kids, a loving husband—too easy! Definitely show gratitude for the big stuff, but know that there is so much more about your life for you to appreciate. In Chapter 11 of *You Have 4 Minutes to Change Your Life*, I wrote about how my dear friend Danny-J, a motivational speaker, taught me the value of being "faithful in the little things," a phrase inspired by a Bible verse in the book of Luke that says, "He who is faithful in what is least is faithful also in much." Looking for the everyday yet often overlooked blessings is a way to show gratitude for the people, things, and circumstances that might feel insignificant at first glance, but in fact make up the contents of our joy.

"The kids are still sleeping." "There's a piece of cheesecake hidden in the fridge." "I have $27 in credit at Target, and it's all mine!" It's as easy as one-two-three. You might find that the little things bring the biggest smiles. Knowing that you have goodness all around can make even the hardest days more bearable. Do you remember my suggestion for journaling away your stress at bedtime? Consider using the pages of the same journal to jot down your gratitude list every day. Reflecting on the feelings of gratitude you woke up with might help balance out whatever you're unloading at night.

Part 3: A Question to Inspire. The work we do on ourselves brings value and benefit to all who surround us. That's who mothers are in this world—beings who are meant to spread love. It's in our nature to be nurturers and leaders, so I think the third part of my morning practice makes total sense. It inspires me to be and do better by asking one simple question, "How can I serve?"

This question is another nod to balance. Part 2 shows us how abundant we already are. There's no doubt that no matter how much you're struggling with in any given moment, there's also room for gratitude. Your "and" statements point to that, too. You are abundant. You are rich in some way. There have been times in my life when I've had a lot of money in the bank and not a financial worry in the world, and plenty of other times when I was looking for loose change to pay for kids' diapers or our next meal. In both circumstances, I had something valuable to give. When I was a young mother with no money, I was still able to help out my single-mom friends by offering to watch their kids for free while they worked. Even if your only currency is the smile on your face, you have something to share with the world. The last part of my prayer is when I ask myself, God, the Universe, "How can I serve?"

The answer is always different, and it comes straight from my intuition. My inner wisdom might say, "Drop off some feminine products at the local women's shelter." The next morning's prayer might offer, "Text 20 people on your contact list and tell them what you appreciate most about them." I always look to three categories to consider how I might be of service to my family, my community, or the world: time, talent, and treasure. How can I give some of my time, offer the benefit of a special talent, or share some of my financial abundance (treasure) with someone else? The answer is usually directly related to one of the gratitude items from Part 2. I refuse to share cheesecake—ever—but I *can* use some leftover balances on gift cards to pick up something for a person in need. Practice this with your kids. Ask them to name three things they're grateful for. Then challenge them to figure out a way to share one of those things with someone else.

Gratitude as Arts and Crafts

When my husband and I were first married and living on a shoe-string budget, we would spend date nights at home doing arts and crafts. My husband happens to be a talented artist and crafts-man and a big sweetheart of a guy, so it was mostly his idea to opt for paint-by-numbers over dinner and a movie. The walls of our home are covered with our creations—cigar-box dioramas, framed portraits of our chickens drawn by our children, and myr-iad other weird and wonderful handmade pieces. Surrounding myself with my family's art makes my heart smile. Looking at it every day reminds me of all I have to love and appreciate.

Teaching kids how to be grateful can be tough. I had to suffer through more than my share of my parents' lectures about starv-ing kids from some far-off place, and I swore I wouldn't do that to my kids (and then I did it anyway). I want my children to appre-ciate what they have and feel a duty to share, but I've struggled with how to do that without guilting them into it. Like me, my kids were born with a strong complaining gene. They each sprang from the womb as expert-level social-justice warriors. Of course, that justice is always a personal crusade for correcting every way the world has already wronged them (yup, even the four-year-old has a long list of injustices levied against her). I hear "But that's not fair" at least 75 trillion times every day before dinner.

The complaining is usually handled with patient listening, a longer age-appropriate conversation when necessary, and the instruction to create their "and" statements. It works *most* of the time, at least in getting them to gain some perspective. All that is a lot of work, though, and not really a lot of fun. Kids don't respond well to un-fun personal-development practices, so I asked my online community to share the ways they teach their kids about gratitude. My favorite answer was one that spoke right to my soul and came from wholistic design expert and color therapist Amy Kate LeRoy—an origami arts and crafts gratitude practice!

Amy's Gratitude Origami

What you'll need:

- Internet access
- Construction paper
- Colorful pens, markers, or crayons
- String or tape
- A place to display your beautiful creations

What you'll do:

- Prepare a short gratitude list with your family.
- Do a quick Internet search for origami patterns and instructions for making your favorite animals, plants, or objects. You're going to create paper sculptures out of your gratitude list!
- On each piece of paper, write one item from your gratitude list.

- Following the instructions you found online, fold your paper into origami sculptures.

Amy suggests making paper birds and hanging them from strings in an area where your family spends a lot of time. Your tiny art sculptures will serve as whimsical celebrations of your family's many blessings. Add new pieces to your display on holidays, birthdays, or the New Year. Taking down a few of the pieces at traditional gifting holidays like Christmas or Hanukkah and coming up with ways to give to others could be a new family tradition centered around gratitude and service. Make the practice your own!

"Loving ourselves works miracles in our lives."
— Louise Hay

Motherhood (womanhood in general) can be a thankless proposition. We can feel beat up at the end of a long day of loving a lot and not receiving much appreciation in return. That's why it's so important to celebrate our blessings and to remember to send love to ourselves, too. When we can balance the not-so-great stuff—and sometimes the personal struggle and heartache—with even a little bit of joy, we reenergize ourselves to do all the big things we were meant to do. We align ourselves with our potential and fuel ourselves for carrying out our purpose. Be grateful that you have been blessed with motherhood, because it means you possess the heart of a nurturer and a capable leader. You have important work to do in this world! Are you ready?

Meditation for Acceptance of What Is

PREPARATION FOR YOUR MEDITATION

Imagine how sweet it would feel to be able to acknowledge the divine lessons that are found in everyday happenings. But we can. When we make room in our lives to receive them, when we accept the obstacles that have been placed in our paths as blessings, when we find peace in a practice of surrender, we are able to feel grateful for all the events that have led us to this present moment. That is the spirit of your Meditation for Acceptance of What Is. What is outside of our control doesn't have to overwhelm or worry us. The unpredictable events of our lives can teach us, reminding us of how much control we have over the reactions to our own circumstances and, ultimately, our happiness.

POSITION / BREATH / GAZE

Find your Easy Seat, choose the breathing technique that will support you in this moment, and prepare to settle into a feeling of peace and ease. This time and space are sacred because you have made it so. You are safe to let go and surrender. You may choose to keep your eyes open, but I always recommend closing them if you can. This helps with removing any visual distraction.

WORDS FOR YOUR PRACTICE

Accept the following words as permission to surrender and to feel supported in this moment. Remember to read them slowly and with an open and receptive heart. Take time to pause between sentences to breathe and to consider the words carefully. Sometimes it helps to read the message more than once before moving on to the mantra portion of the meditation. Do whatever feels good to you.

Surrender is the gift you give yourself when control fails to serve you. Discernment is a practice rooted in wisdom and self-love. Letting go is the expression of understanding what is and is not yours to hold and releasing what doesn't belong to you.

Taking on what isn't yours will only result in struggle and hopelessness. If it isn't yours, you're not meant to hold it. When you find that you're overwhelmed by responsibility, worry, and the weight of all you've taken on, can you love yourself enough to let some of it go?

Letting go of what doesn't serve you makes space for more goodness in your life. As you let go of what isn't yours, blessings and lessons will come from all directions.

Let go and look for the lessons. Surrender and feel the weight of worry being lifted from your weary spirit. Be grateful and watch as the Universe rewards you with even more blessings. Accept what is, and know that life is happening for you, not to you.

Making space and expressing gratitude for all that you already have makes you ready and worthy to receive infinite blessings.

YOUR MANTRA

Bring your attention to your breath. Follow your easy inhales and exhales until you fall into a rhythm of even and effortless breath cycles. Read your mantra silently to yourself or out loud in a whisper before closing your eyes. Stay with your breath, repeating your mantra on each exhale, until you feel fully relaxed and ready to return to your day.

*I am wise, I am grateful, and I am ready to hold
and receive all the good that's meant for me.*

Phase 3

CRACKING
OPEN

CHAPTER 7

TINY SEEDS AND BIG DREAMS

The 25-minute drive to my older sister Danielle's house for Sunday family dinner takes us through the countryside and past at least a dozen farm stands. As summer ends and we usher in the shorter days of autumn, rows of potted mums, gourds, and trays of decorative grasses replace crates of fruits and vegetables. The evergreens and vibrant reds and oranges of the flowers remind me of my mother's garden, one she spent countless hours designing and manicuring, one that won her awards and spotlights in local newspapers. The backyard of my childhood home was tiny, less than 450 square feet, but my mother's talent was giant.

Passing one of the stands on a recent Sunday afternoon, I sighed and said to my husband, "I'll never be as good at gardening as my mother was." I pictured our sad, raggedy garden boxes that have lain vacant since we built them nearly five years ago. "You can learn to do anything," my husband assured me. "Let's clean up the boxes. We can start small with just a few plants. It'll be fun!" That immediately conjured memories of my mother's first garden. She was cleaning up the house after her divorce from my father, and our overgrown backyard (a source of embarrassment for practically my whole life) got a mini-makeover. She mowed the high grass, threw out the debris and long-abandoned toys, and carved out a tiny bed in the corner. It was just big enough for a small evergreen bush and a few flowers. She was so proud of that little plot! It's almost incredible to imagine what it eventually grew to become.

And then it occurred to me—I was 10 when my father moved out of the house, which means my mother was 40, the same age I am now. She was my age when she discovered an entirely new passion. She was a 40-year-old single mother of three children, living in a run-down house on the very limited income of a small-town grocery store produce manager. And she made a decision to rebuild her life with whatever was available to her, no matter how long it took.

My mother's aspirations were small, and her wants were few. She wanted a clean, pretty home where she might finally be happy. And she wanted a creative outlet that made her feel like she was meant for more than just working and taking care of children. Step-by-step, one half-price sad little bush at a time, my mother created a paradise out of a postage-sized patch of weeds and rocky soil. I can see it all now—her vision, her plan, and the wisdom of her patient execution.

I said before that my mother had incredible talent—giant, even. While it's true that her natural talent was something to be admired, it's her process that inspires me now. She died 25 years after starting her garden, and she was still working to improve upon it right up until the last days of her life. Her work would never be finished. She was constantly updating her vision, taking small steps to make it happen, and enjoying every single step of the journey.

Isn't that something we all want? Wouldn't it be lovely to have a dream, go after it with belief, enthusiasm, and persistence, and feel joyful in every moment along the way?

As mothers, our shared *negative* habit is to take on much more responsibility than we can handle with proper attention to both the task and our health. And because our perception is often that there's not enough time or opportunity to go around, we clamor at ourselves to get everything on our to-do list done in an unreasonable time frame and attach ourselves to *every* opportunity that comes our way. Worse, when we do say no, or an option is closed off to us, we feel like we've failed or missed our chance for happiness, growth, success, love, dreams . . . the list goes on.

These are worries born in a misunderstanding of how dreams are actually realized. Practical manifestation, Divine Discernment, and compassionate goal-setting will be the theme of this part of the book. Your practice will be to learn how to identify and take action on the right messages, responsibilities, and opportunities that are meant for you in any given moment.

Like my mother, we all have the chance to create dreams that inspire. In this chapter, we'll look at how to find and use proper scheduling tools to nurture those dreams. Through this work, you'll be able to build confidence for the next phase, which is all about taking action. Growing up, we are often so focused on what our mothers fail to do that we neglect the beautiful gardens they're growing beneath our feet. Let's not do that to ourselves. We can make those dreams come true and still manage the mayhem and messiness of everyday mom life. All we have to do is look to our own mothers (or the great examples of motherhood around us) to see how much that's true.

For the Late Bloomer

I actually don't believe in *late* bloomers. Flowers bloom precisely when they're meant to. Of course, it's important that the seeds be planted in good ground and that the seedlings be fed and watered properly. But when a flower decides to bloom isn't up to anyone but the flower. Creating drama over the punctuality of a bloom doesn't serve any good purpose. It certainly doesn't speed up the growing process. Bringing a flower to full bloom is a dance of nurturing and allowing. It's up to you to plant the seeds in healthy soil and to make sure adequate food, water, and sunlight are available, but the growing and blooming parts aren't yours to control (or worry about). And yet, we women persist in our attempts to control the process of our own blooming and worry about when and if it's ever going to happen. It's a practice that frustrates the spirit and creates unnecessary anxiety.

"I've always been a late bloomer, so I never feel like, 'Oh, I'm gettin' older; I guess everything is gonna stop.' I'm the opposite. 'Oh, I'm just getting started.'"
— Megan Mullally

There are also the flowers that bloom with no help from us at all—the wildflowers. The unexpected beauty of their blossoms sprinkles the landscape with magic. Although they grow just like weeds, we decide that they're valuable because they please our eye. We pick them and bring them inside to admire them up close. The wildflowers' seeds were planted not with careful hands, but by the wind carrying them through the air or creatures dropping them in their travels. Think about the wildflowers that have sprouted up across the landscape of your life. Did you count them among your blessings, or did you dismiss them as weeds? Were you able to love your wildflowers even though you didn't *intentionally* plant the seeds?

Begin Again

It was the summer of 2010, and I was in Tara Stiles' first Strala yoga guide training in New York City. The classes took place all day Saturday and Sunday, so I was spending the weekends in my younger sister Leah's Brooklyn apartment to be closer to the Strala studio. It was turning out to be a magical summer filled with yoga, new friends, a little taste of freedom, and what felt like a new beginning for me. The weekdays in between were when I got busy vlogging (video blogging) all about the experience on my then-young YouTube channel and practicing my vinyasa yoga class plans with my friends and personal training clients. I was on an adventure of creating a new phase of my life, and it was all happening at my favorite time of the year. I celebrated my 32nd birthday at the studio in July. Everything was perfect at home and in my budding professional life.

I realized nearly one month into the training, during a phone call with Leah, that I hadn't gotten my period the whole time. I wasn't upset or complaining. Honestly, it was super convenient to not be crampy and bleeding while having to balance upside down in yoga pants—but my sister thought I should take a pregnancy test, just in case. I didn't believe for a second that I might be pregnant. But there I was, alone with the kids while Justin was on a job with our only car, when Leah rushed to the local pharmacy and showed up at my house with a pregnancy test 15 minutes later.

Two pink lines. *Neon* pink lines. It was like I was *super* pregnant. Justin and I had discussed many times the possibility of having children of our own. But we already had the three older kids from my first marriage, and that felt like enough. Our lives were happy and full. We had time just for us almost every weekend when the kids went to their dad's house. Romantic getaways were easy and frequent, and we had time to discover new interests. All the kids were in school and exploring their own activities and budding independence. We had three kids, but we also got to have a lot of just-adult fun and were enjoying a growing sense of freedom. Having more kids was something we sometimes fantasized about, but we had ultimately decided it wouldn't be best for our family. Seeing two pink lines gave way to panic, not excitement.

I sent my sister home and decided to call Justin right away. Waiting for him to get back from work to tell him would have been unbearable. Staring out into my backyard with my elbows resting on my kitchen windowsill, I waited nervously for him to pick up his phone. The call went something like this:

"Hello?" Justin answered.

"Hey, where are you?" I asked.

"I'm on my way home. I pulled over at a rest stop to take a quick nap before getting back on the road."

"Oh, good. Don't drive when you're tired."

"I won't."

"Hey, I need to tell you something," I began.

"Yeah?"

"I got something."

"What?"

"Guess."

"You got something . . . A job?" Justin asked innocently.

"No."

"I don't know. I'm tired. Tell me."

"Pregnant. I got pregnant."

Without skipping a beat, my husband replied, "I'm grabbing a coffee. I'll be home in forty-five minutes."

By the time he got home from his 45-minute car ride, Justin was already a proud and doting father. All of my anxiety in that moment was centered on his previous statements about not wanting more children. I had usually been the one who brought up the conversation about maybe having another, and he was the one who had dismissed it as impractical. I was sure he'd be upset or at least slow to jump on board, so I was completely thrown off by his exuberance. There I was, feeling alone with an overflowing bag of mixed emotions. He was celebrating, and I was like a half-deflated birthday balloon, a sad leftover from a party that ended too soon. This was my first pregnancy after I'd gotten happy—after I was no longer in an abusive marriage or confused about who I was or what I was meant to do in this world. I felt like I had finally figured out my life and was ready to bloom. A baby, I knew, would turn everything upside down.

It doesn't feel good to share this. So many women struggle with fertility, and I don't want to seem ungrateful or trigger any painful emotional responses in women reading this. If you've ever had trouble conceiving or are still on that journey, I honor and hold space for you and your heartache. That tiny zygote that created so much personal drama is now my sweet, brilliant seven-year-old, Sunny. I wouldn't change anything about how he came into our lives, even the messy, confusing parts.

Turning the Soil

That's the nature of life, though—things sometimes have to be turned upside down for new and better things to emerge. In *Women Who Run with the Wolves*, Clarissa Pinkola Estés, Ph.D., reminds us of how the garden soil must be turned over in fall to be suitable for plants to bloom in spring. Even when our plans are intentionally made—when we are mindfully planting the seeds to bring forward exactly what we desire—turning a situation upside down or destroying something is part of the process. I was planting seeds with my yoga training, building an online community, and practicing personal development, but I wasn't letting go of anything to make room for my biggest dreams—I was doing *all* the things instead of only what would truly serve my goals. I hadn't turned over the soil or allowed for the part of my journey that called for destruction.

To be clear, destruction doesn't necessarily mean bad or painful. Destruction can mean letting go of a tightly held idea or old habit. It's critical to intellectual, emotional, and spiritual growth. This pregnancy had blindsided me, but I couldn't let it derail me. I had to let go of the idea that my blooming had a deadline and that the path to success had to look a certain way. I had to say to myself, "Dreams don't need perfect conditions or specific timelines to come true. There are many paths to where you want to go." I needed to destroy old opinions to give way to the life I wanted. In order to move forward, I had to let go of the idea that the seeds I was planting were the only way to make my garden beautiful.

I also needed to allow for the weather and the wind that would carry the seeds of the wildflowers and weeds. I had to teach myself to practice allowing and discernment. I had made a plan, and God laughed. I planted seeds, and the wind said, "Wait just a minute. I have something to add here." I was forced to step back from the busyness of planting, dust the dirt off my hands and knees, and make a conscious choice about which seeds I would and wouldn't nurture. My baby was a wildflower seed dropped by the wind that I made room for by letting go of whatever would crowd him out. I finished my training, but I only continued leading yoga classes until he was born. I poured more energy into my online platform, which allowed me more time to be home with him. I said no to opportunities that didn't fit in with my life as the mother of a newborn. Each one of us can learn how to create a dream and choose which opportunities to nurture. Mastering that process is what brings dreams to life. And it's at the root of V = P – O. By removing the obstacles to my own joy, I was able to turn the pressure of a new and unexpected life into a new source of vitality (and let's face it, exhaustion).

That process is the true nature of physical manifestation.

Digging for Gold

Erin Stutland is a fitness expert, a TV show host, and a new mom. She also happens to be the creator of one of the most soul-nourishing workouts on the planet, Shrink Session, and the author of *Mantras in Motion: Manifesting What You Want through Mindful Movement*. It was at the end of one of her live Shrink Session classes in New York City that she sat the whole class down and challenged us to write a list of our greatest desires. Back then, she called it a gold-digger list, but I refer to it as a *Goal*-Digger List. It's been five years since I took that class, and the list still lives in the notes section of my phone.

A timer was set, and we got to work. Erin instructed us to start each statement with "I want." It was electrifying to release my desires into the world (or at least into my phone). In the spirit of raw vulnerability, I'm going to show you my unedited list. *Spoiler alert*: There's a happy ending. Almost every single thing on this list has come true. And that is precisely why I have to share it. Manifesting—when done intentionally and in a spirit of flexibility and belief and with a willingness to take action—works.

I also want to note that this is an old list. My old desires have evolved, and I can easily list 1,000 new desires that reflect my personal growth and current aspirations. When I wrote this, I was focused on my business. Now, I would include more about relationships and how I want to impact the world through activism and philanthropy. The most important thing was that I made a list. It didn't have to be the list to end all lists. Your list will be a jumping-off point for you, too.

MY GOAL-DIGGER LIST

- I want to spend money on the tools I need to build my business.
- I want to buy clothes that will make me look professional and grown-up.
- I want to take more classes and not be afraid to look like I don't know how to do something.
- I want to showcase my expertise on a bigger scale.
- I want a TV show.
- I want to be the leader in the projects I'm a part of.
- I want to be fearless when I ask for money for my services.
- I want to know I'm worth it.
- I want to feel like I deserve to have success.
- I want others to feel like I deserve to have success based on what I've done, not what people have given me.
- I want to be well-respected by my peers.

- I want to be invited to do more projects.
- I want to be fearless when asking for favors and interviews and collaborations.
- I want to look on the outside how I feel about myself on the inside.
- I want more money for the work I do.
- I want to stand up for myself and say no when business partners ask too much of me.
- I want to be a better partner and friend.
- I want everyone I work with to leave with a sense that they got their money's worth.
- I want to speak about my passion, not about what I think is popular.
- I want to do good work and have people love it.
- I want to continue to build amazing relationships and friendships with peers and colleagues.

DECLARING YOUR WANTS

Now, it's your turn. Set a timer for five minutes and write your own Goal-Digger List. Declare your desire for the million-dollar home, the relationship of your dreams, the super-slide trampoline pool! (Okay, maybe that's another one for my list.) Begin every statement with "I want," and don't be shy about any of it. This is the first step in creating your Grand Vision. The next step is revisiting your previous work and expanding upon all the magic you've already made.

She Turned Her Dreams into Plans

Children aren't the only things raised with a balance of nature and nurture. Your dreams are also born and brought to maturity using the same. Nature provides the soil, the wind, the rain, and the sun. It also brings the weeds, the wildflowers, and the creatures just looking for a free meal. These manifest in your life as opportunities, luck, helpful and hurtful people, and supportive and challenging circumstances. You are the nurture part of this process. You ready the soil by turning it over and adding nutrients and fertilizer, you position your garden where it will receive the right amount of sunlight, you protect it from pests and animals, you pull invasive weeds, and you water it when rainfall is insufficient. In terms of nurturing your dreams, this means taking action steps that support your goals, knowing which opportunities to take and which to leave alone, and calling in assistance from others when your efforts (or just a belief that things will work out) is insufficient.

Just to be clear, I'm a huge fan of prayer and meditation, but they're merely early steps in the manifestation process. Action is always required for manifesting the life you want. I also want to state something that's obvious, but not said enough: there are situations beyond our control that can't be easily worked out with positive affirmations and action steps from your favorite personal-development coach. Taking action isn't always appropriate or possible.

Death, divorce, poverty, mental or physical illness—that's all real stuff that can make just functioning day-to-day feel impossible. When I lost both my parents in 2013, I went numb. I didn't integrate my pain into my plan or carefully and meticulously weed my garden to make room for new things to grow. I let the whole damn garden wither and die. I shut down. Job opportunities and contracts fell by the wayside, relationships were neglected, and I went into a long, cold winter of the spirit. I realize that at one time you might have been or might currently be in a space like that. And you might have far fewer resources than I do, resources that made for a softer landing when I fell. Just know this—after winter comes spring. This is nature's promise. Always.

Allow yourself to sit in your dark place for a while if that's what you need. Every gardener needs rest. Every garden, after having been turned over, needs time to break down the plants and reabsorb nutrients into its soil. You need time to recharge and reintegrate, too. Just make sure you're doing it safely, supported by people you love and trust and with the intention to return to the world. If it feels too dark and scary, get help. Collaboration—with community members, friends and family, and sometimes trusted mental-health professionals—has always been my greatest source of strength. Everything I've ever built has been done with the help of others. There isn't one part of me that's self-made. Growing my garden took a village!

Having a clear Grand Vision is so important. Dreaming is a practice that I don't approach lightly. I'm a curious and distracted wanderer by nature, so it takes very little to guide me off-course. I'll chase a shiny object or a fluttering butterfly anywhere. While my path isn't set in stone, having a richly detailed vision that excites and inspires me is the easiest way to sort out which opportunities to pursue and how to handle aspects of my life that aren't fully in my control. My Grand Vision helps me decide what to pick up, what to put down, and what to leave for someone else. I have a couple of fun tools and an easy crafts project (you know how much I love making stuff) to help you write about and support a vision that excites and inspires *you*.

Expanding on a Dream

In Chapter 5, you wrote about your future, and I hope you wove a little fantasy into your story. Now, it's time to expand on that effort by integrating your Goal-Digger List into your future story, creating a brand-new dream scene that will guide your next steps. Meditation is going to be a big part of this activity, so get ready to go deep within to call on those big, beautiful desires.

Step 1: How does it feel? Review your Goal-Digger List (page 107) and Step 3 from "The Story of You" (page 77). Read what you wrote slowly and with reverence. Check in with how you're feeling in your body as you read. Notice if anything you wrote elicits a pang of discomfort or a twinge of excitement. Paying attention to how ideas *feel* in your body is an important aspect of practicing Divine Discernment. It helps to sort out what's good and what's not so good for you.

Step 2: Meditate on it. Close your eyes (if that feels comfortable and safe) or pick a spot in the room to place your gaze softly upon. Recall your list and story. How would those elements manifest as a perfect day in your future? Imagine yourself waking up on that day. What sights, sounds, and circumstances are present? Seek out the details as your Perfect Future Day unfolds. Who is with you? Where do you go? What pleasurable things do you do throughout the day? Feel into each moment, checking in and noticing any physical sensations or responses. Sit in this meditation for just a short time or for as long as you'd like. As soon as your Perfect Future Day is clear, open your eyes and proceed to the next step.

Step 3: Write it down. Write in great detail about what came up during your meditation. It might be easier to make a bullet-point list of all the parts of your Perfect Future Day instead of telling it as a story. I always record my thoughts in writing because I believe it's one of the best ways to breathe life into our ideas. Writing isn't everyone's cup of tea, though, and it might not be yours. If this is true for you, consider creating a video diary or recording your thoughts on your phone. Or, if you want to get super bold with this practice, share your thoughts in a vlog (that's how I started my online platform).

Your Perfect Future Day is one of the biggest and most important parts of your Grand Vision. It's a tool that you'll use again and again to keep yourself on track to achieving your goals and as a reminder of the feelings and experiences you *really* want to call in. Keep your description handy for future work.

Your Vision in Words and Pictures

Shortly after we moved into our home in 2012, Justin gifted me an inspiration board to hang in my home office. He made it from an old, ornate picture frame he found out with someone's trash at the curb, adding red lacquer spray paint and some self-adhesive cork he picked up at a home-improvement store. One of the first things I pinned to it was a badge I had received from the Hay House Writer's Workshop I attended in 2013. I added the title of "published author" under my name, even though it would still be a few years before I accomplished such a feat. It was at that workshop that I stood up to ask one of my favorite authors, Kris Carr, a question, and she told the audience that I "sparkled." I've always wanted to sparkle, and the fact that a personal hero saw that in me made me more aware of my magic. Never doubt the power we can have on others!

Attending the writer's workshop was in perfect alignment with my future dream. I knew I was going to write a book, even though I still had no idea what it would be about. Claiming that I would be a published author didn't feel audacious or premature. My heart knew it was inevitable because I could see it in my Grand Vision, and I was already putting my plan in motion just by showing up at the workshop. That was one of the first steps. Many more followed and led me down a path right to my dream publisher's office, where I presented my first book proposal. I actually waddled into the office, seven months pregnant with my fifth baby.

Kris Carr would end up writing the foreword for my first book, a dream realized. That's the not-so-magical magic of manifesting—create a dream, hold the vision and the belief that it's possible, say yes to opportunities that support your vision, take action, and repeat. But more on that later.

I also pinned love notes from friends, motivational messages, and images cut from magazines or printed off the Internet to my inspiration board. The only criterion for what made it onto the board was that it support some aspect of my Grand Vision. My board is still positioned right above my work desk, where I can look at it every day. Every note, affirmation, and image serve as a reminder of my goals and where I'm intentionally headed. As milestones are met and new goals are set, I rearrange my board and add fresh inspiration.

Creating your own inspiration board doesn't have to be expensive or complicated. It can be as simple as picking up a $10 magnetic whiteboard from Target (a.k.a. the happiest place on Earth) or recycling an old picture frame like my husband did for mine. Once you have your board, hang it in a place you'll visit often. Keep reminders of your big dreams front and center to stay connected to your goals, and allow the reminders to inspire you to take action. Know that with tiny but intentional steps taken every day, you can have anything your heart truly desires. You are capable of creating your own happiness. Don't let yourself forget that.

CHAPTER 8

HOW TO MAKE TIME FOR WHAT MATTERS

When my oldest child went back to college for her junior year, she left her hamster behind—a "gift" for the little kids. I'm going to admit something right off the bat that I'm not very proud of: The hamster lived in the spare bedroom for a week before I knew it was there. You read that right—a rodent was living in my house for seven whole days, my six-year-old and three-year-old were taking care of it, and I didn't have a clue!

In my defense, I'm going to remind you that Kevin McCallister's mother in *Home Alone* was halfway to Paris before she realized he wasn't with them. Okay fine, she was a fictional mom in a comedy, but all comedy is based in some reality, right? Right? With five kids, two adults, and I don't know how many animals occupying one space, there have been many days when my house felt more like Grand Central Station than a moderate-size family home. It's loud and rarely still. Doors are always opening and closing, and there's no telling who might be walking in—family, friends, one of my workshop participants (I run a learning space out of my house, too). Our home is chaotic and wonderful, and apparently runs so well on its own that rodents can live for weeks at a time without parental knowledge.

There are moments when I take a step back and marvel at all the activity happening under one roof. Tiny people and tinier creatures, young adults, and my husband and me, all scurrying around to whatever meeting or practice, yelling from room to room, and battling for shower time. We're a busy crew. We do a lot. And somehow, we don't suffer for it. Oh, we're tired at the end of the day. I don't want you to think any of it is easy or doesn't take effort. But my husband and I end most days feeling really tired, really good, and frequently with a preschooler passed out between us, tablet in hand.

I told you in the first lines of this book that getting all the important stuff done and finding gratitude in the messiness of motherhood starts with letting go . . . and still being able to accomplish everything you want. I know how ridiculous that sounds, especially when (you can't see this, but . . .) I have no less than four loads of laundry blanketing my laundry-room floor right now, and I might be wearing the same sweatpants for the third day in a row. I will show you how to make time for laundry, soccer practice, *and* making your dreams come true. I swear on my secret stash of chocolate-covered espresso beans!

This is the part of our journey together where we take a look at the nitty-gritty of your everyday life. You're going to figure out what's stressing you out and weighing you down (sometimes unnecessarily) so you can tackle the stuff that's running you ragged during the day and keeping you up at night. I want you to be able to go to bed like I do—feeling good about my day and myself. And that requires release.

In this chapter, we'll explore three stages of release that are going to require you to challenge some popular beliefs and even some stories you've made up yourself. Whether it's conventional media, social media, friends, or the local crunchy mom crew, we're overwhelmed with messages about what motherhood *should* look like and how we're supposed to be handling it (in Instagrammable matching mint-and-gold outfits). Most of the messages are suitable only for the trash can. "Supposed to" might be the most dangerous thing you can say to a struggling mom. At best, it's not helpful. At worst, it can make her feel hopelessly inadequate.

Here's what you get to do right now:

- Release the idea that it's all up to you.
- Release the idea that it's all *for* you.
- Release the idea that it all has to be done right now.

Take a deep breath and prepare yourself for some epic letting-go. Picture Beyoncé in *Lemonade*, fires blazing behind her, a baseball bat in her hand, and a glorious look of satisfaction on her face. Prepare to be liberated, sister!

Release the Idea that It's All Up to You

You are doing a great job. I know that without even having met you. You've made it more than halfway through this book, which is more than most individuals can say about their reading habits. You're here, learning how to show up better in motherhood. You're someone who strives for excellence not just because you love your children, but because you love yourself. I feel you, because I strive for the same—and love my children just as much.

But here's another truth: You're not excellent at everything, and that's okay.

Let's bring it back to the hamster story for a minute. There I was, a woman totally in control of her life, shooting for excellence in every area, from how I ran my business to how I folded my family's laundry. On one hand, I get huge gratification from my strong work ethic and what it can teach my kids. For example, my 15-year-old recently shared with me that he's been folding his pants the way I showed him, and he can't believe how neatly and flatly they fit into his dresser. This validation shot through my system like an electrical jolt. I was giddy for the rest of the day!

Something can also be learned from releasing the need for excellence and control. My little girls were taking care of a living animal in my house for a week, and I was none the wiser. I could be embarrassed by that (and I am a little), but here's an "and" statement for you: I had no idea there was a hamster in my house, *and* my children proved themselves to be responsible, caring people who know how to take care of important tasks on their own. Something in my house got done well and without my help, input, or guidance. Imagine that!

Harvesting Lessons from Loss

It took extreme circumstances to really wake me up and make me release some control. It all started in the summer of 2015. Work and family stress, mounting health issues, and the pressure I was putting on myself to handle it all had sent me into a rapid decline that was spiraling out of control. My period was slowly becoming heavier and less regular, and I was gaining weight out of nowhere with no change in my diet (which has always been pretty healthy). I started experiencing pain all over my body, especially in my joints, and white spots (caused by a condition called vitiligo) started appearing on my face, neck, and torso. All of this freaked me out, but it didn't compel me to take much action. I had too much work to do and too many people to take care of! I put myself last.

Over the next two and a half years, I would grow my business, publish my first book, suffer massively painful shifts in my family dynamics, and go through some really hard financial times. I did end up seeing a bunch of doctors and getting lots of tests, but my efforts to follow up with specialists were half-assed at best. I was just spread too thin, and I wasn't asking for help. All that ended in December 2017, when I experienced a devastating miscarriage.

Before you read any further, I want you to know that I don't blame myself for the miscarriage I suffered, or any other woman for one she has experienced. Pregnancy loss is terrible but common, and we rarely know the cause. It's one of those awful parts of motherhood that none of us want to face but too many of us know as our reality. The one positive that did come out of it was that I decided that I could no longer ignore my health. I still don't have a concrete diagnosis, but I do have an excellent team of doctors and wellness professionals helping me feel better every day.

Losing my pregnancy was long and painful. I chose to move through and feel the process fully instead of using medical options to speed it up or ease the pain. This was a personal, spiritual decision I made for myself. It's not one I recommend, but we all choose our own paths through pain—and that was mine. It's important that you choose health-care practices that work for you and that are guided by professionals you know and trust. I stayed in my bedroom for seven days and nights, and because it's hard for me to revisit what I was feeling in that moment, I'll share what I wrote on social media on my first day out of bed.

I emerged from my room this morning after a week of working, eating, sleeping, crying, praying, FaceTiming, texting, aching, laughing, Netflixing, mourning, and birthing in my bed.

My baby was only with me for a short time, but this was a birth—not so different from the five that produced children I still get to hold.

Yesterday, while drifting in and out of sleep, I imagined my baby tucked inside the dark, warm cave my body creates when I sleep on my side, curled up in a ball. This is how I slept with all my babies, nursing them through the night. I breathed in the scent of her head and felt her soft, warm belly against mine.

So, this is how I know she exists. That this happened. And that this was birth.

As I made my way into my laundry room this morning and started tidying what had been disrupted during my week upstairs, I thought about the wholeness of this experience and the wholeness of me. I've been bleeding for seven days, and during that time a torrent of consciousness moved through me, forcing forward every emotion, revealing every old story, and carrying with it strength and wisdom unknown to me before now.

Teachers and healers often get the advice to wait to tell the story of a thing until they've landed on the side of healing. I understand the wisdom of that, but it only really applies if you're delivering answers. And I'm not a deliverer of answers. I'm just a storyteller. That's my way.

And this isn't something I'll get over. I'll always be moving through it, as I am with all the hurt and struggle I've ever experienced. I'm always moving through it, though with greater ease as time passes, and I'm always telling the story of that.

I'm still bleeding this morning. My body still hurts. My heart still aches. And I'm also happy, and hopeful, and filled with excitement for things to learn and actions to take in the new year.

I'm recognizing fully the wholeness and beauty of this "breaking," even through the grief—BECAUSE of the grief. What a blessing it is to feel so many things, to be gifted with so many learning experiences, to feel such big hurts and overwhelming joys in one life—in one short week.

A single lightning bolt can light up what a thousand lanterns cannot. And a single moment and a lifetime both have the same potential to enlighten.

As the learning continues, I'll keep telling the stories. You can take what you like or find useful from whatever I share and leave the rest. That's a good practice to apply to all things (and the only advice I'll give).

And as a request, I'd like you to take a moment to recognize the wholeness of YOU, and all the many moments of breaking and layers of learning that make your wisdom so abundant—and beautiful.

Something else magical happened during that time that I wasn't expecting. I learned to *really* let go of the idea that everything was up to me. Of course, there were other times when I was stuck in bed sick or I had to travel for work, and my anxiety would go into overdrive thinking about all the things that were being done "wrong" in my absence. This time was different. I let my husband take care of me, the kids, and whatever else needed to be done. I checked out of the busyness of the world and into my body and my feelings.

Because of my ongoing health issues, I already had been slowly releasing control. Justin had taken over big tasks like managing our health insurance, doctor appointments, and taxes. After my miscarriage, though, I no longer felt anxiety about letting him do any of it. I came to realize that there are times that call for our full surrender. I had been forced to learn the hard way—when I lost my parents, when I was having a hard time with postpartum anxiety, when I needed time to make and go to doctor's appointments—that my lack of full surrender in the past only prolonged and worsened my suffering.

You might not have the luxury of abundant help or finances to be able to check out for long periods of time, but can you fully surrender for even just a moment in one aspect of your life? Is it possible to duck away for a short meditation or opt for frozen dinners once in a while instead of making a home-cooked meal? And how many things are you claiming responsibility for? Micromanaging, taking on more despite your overwhelmingly busy schedule, or refusing to recognize that something can be handled competently by somebody else (and guess what, it can)? I bet the answer is "a lot." And I realize that you might not have a partner or family close by to pick up the slack for you. I'm going to address how to navigate those circumstances, too. But I do know that taking on every responsibility yourself is not serving you at all (or anyone else, for that matter).

"When you're passionate about something, you want it to be all it can be. But in the endgame of life, I fundamentally believe the key to happiness is letting go of that idea of perfection."
— Debra Messing

Just to give you some deeper insight, here's a short list of things I didn't allow anyone but myself to handle for the first 37 years of my life (with the exception of my mother, who taught me the "right" way to do almost everything—see the tree, see the freshly fallen apple sitting right next to it):

- Loading the dishwasher
- Folding the laundry
- Paying bills
- Filling out school forms
- Filling out health forms
- Organizing the closets
- Keeping the family calendar
- Planning birthday parties
- Writing holiday gift lists
- Etcetera, etcetera, etcetera (Any *The King and I* fans in the house?)

Did you see yourself at all in my list? Which areas of your life could use a little less control and a lot more surrender? Challenge yourself to name at least five tasks you can delegate to someone else. I promise you that just *imagining* what it would be like to let go of a little responsibility will feel amazing. Picture a neatly (or semi-neatly—let's keep it real here) folded pile of clean clothes that required none of your time or emotional labor (laundry is serious business!). Imagine your partner coming home with a present and a card for your child's classmate's birthday party; you don't even know what the present is because it's already wrapped, and you don't care! Talk about a turn-on. Go ahead and try it out for yourself.

Use this space to list five tasks you're willing to let someone else help with or handle.

1. _____

_____

2. _____

_____

3. _____

_____

4. _____

_____

5. _____

_____

The Problem with Perfection

I became a prisoner of my own ideas of perfection. I believed there was a right way to do everything, and that if I wanted something done right, I had to do it myself. That means I assigned myself every task, big and small. Taking care of my household, my family, and my business overwhelmed and exhausted me, but I couldn't let even one small piece of it go. And when I did let someone else take care of anything at all, I would micromanage the entire process.

If you've ever refolded a bath towel after someone else tried to do it for you, you might be suffering from the same affliction. I remember my mother coming home one day and refolding every towel in the linen closet after I had just finished folding and putting them all away with pride and a sense of accomplishment in my heart. I was 11 years old, and her reaction crushed me. And then, I became a mother who did that to her kids, too.

Today I can empathize with my mother. I know that wanting things to be perfect doesn't make us bad. It took me a long time to give up my attachment to perfection because it made me feel safe when so much of my life seemed out of control. My need to do everything myself wasn't because my family was doing anything fundamentally "wrong." Doing things "right" was how I earned positive attention as a child and how I coped with the chaos of a broken home. I equate perfect order with love and safety, so being what I considered perfect and creating perfect conditions were ways I showed my family how much I loved them. It was how I made myself feel worthy of their love.

There was one big problem with connecting perfection with love or worth, though. Perfection is a myth, and the pursuit of it can break the spirit. Seeking perfection was a fruitless effort that always led to frustration and disappointment. Striving to *be* perfect myself led to feelings of failure. Can we decide together right now that perfection is something we don't need or want and admit that the desire for it is actually hurting us?

Look, I don't expect you to release your perfectionist tendencies overnight. I sure didn't. No one does. Truth be told, I still don't let anyone else in my laundry room—keeping that environment neat and clean is one of the ways I manage my anxiety. But I have found ways to release the pressure I was putting on myself. More on that soon!

Release the Idea that It's All *for* You

"You can have it all."

"You can have it all, but not all at once."

"You can have it all, but not all at once, and your family is probably going to suffer because of it."

"You can have it all, but do you even want it all?"

Talk about mixed messages! If you're anything like me—and I bet you are just by virtue of the fact that you're reading this book—you are multitalented, you have many interests, and you want to accomplish big things in this life. You see yourself as being more than just a mother, and you want to explore all those other parts of yourself that are still undiscovered. You want to birth your Grand Vision! But you're exhausted, and your calendar is running out of space, and that mom guilt is taking over, making you feel like you should be home and not out pursuing your dreams. Hearing conflicting messages about what aspirations we can and should hold as women doesn't help. In fact, it's what has continued to hold us back for generations.

There is a message among the ones listed above that I do use quite regularly to bring myself back to my Grand Vision: "You can have it all, but do you even want it all?" I like questions like this because they call on me to reexamine my own ideas and inspire me to make up my own rules.

I've been doing this personal-development work for a long time, so I've written about my fantasy dream life a bazillion times. My dream scene used to look something like this:

> Justin and I have been happily married for 30 years, and we live in a beach house in California. Our children and grand-children visit us all the time, and we take luxurious family vacations every year. I've written several *New York Times* bestsellers, and I travel all over the world for large speaking engagements. I get invited to all of Oprah's big events and even get to go to her private home for interviews and parties. I'm in the best shape of my life and having the best sex of my life, and I wake up every day feeling vibrant and excited to take on a new day.

Sounds amazing, right? Who wouldn't want *that* life? There was one big issue with it, though. It sounded great, but it wasn't my dream. It was actually a dream I thought I *should* want, based on the dreams of my friends, colleagues, and random strangers on social media. After I learned how to declare and feel into desires of my own, I had to reexamine my dream by affirming that I could have it all, but also asking myself if any of it was what I really wanted.

So, while I definitely want to be married to my husband forever, whether or not my children have their own children is totally up to them. I'm happy with the family I already have. I like the beach just fine, but I can't swim and have a fear of open water. Being a *New York Times* best-selling author would be amazing, but I'm incredibly grateful that my words are out in the world at all. Already having two books that I've poured my heart and soul into feels like more than enough. Nix traveling for work. Yes to parties with Oprah. I want to be healthy and pain-free, but I also know that I can be happy with a chronic illness, too—there's no pressure to make my body or my health perfect. Sex is great—keep *that* on the list. Then, add strong friendships with women I love and respect, a cozy cottage in the woods (or maybe a sprawling ranch house in the desert—or both!), a learning space where I can guide small groups of women through healing workshops and rituals, and an Airstream trailer that my husband and I will use to visit every national park and wacky roadside attraction in America. Top it all off with piles of colorful muumuus, all the vegan ice cream and gluten-free pizza I can eat, and wild, soulful, honest expression in every area of my life, and *that* feels more like my *real* dream. And the kids! I almost forgot about the kids! That's because while my husband and I are living it up—all wild and free on the road—my kids are all following paths to beautiful, fulfilling lives of their own (which they will happily hit the pause button on to visit us every Christmas).

Social and traditional media, advertisements, and our families, friends, and peers are constantly telling us what we can and can't have and what we should and shouldn't want. Wouldn't it feel good to just decide for yourself what actually makes you happy and go for more of *that*?

Through your work in Chapter 3, you should now have more tools to tap in to your intuition with greater ease. As I mentioned in Chapter 4, my friend Elizabeth DiAlto guides women to connect with the physical feelings in their bodies rather than utilizing their intellects to find answers to their biggest questions. Let's try this simple exercise from Elizabeth and see how it feels!

Step 1: Start a blank page or note (preferably in the same place you're keeping the rest of the work from this book).

Step 2: Create three columns and write "Wild Dreams and Desires" at the top of the first column, "Really, Why?" at the top of the second column, and "The Truth" at the top of the third column.

Step 3: Now, take at least three deep breaths. With each inhale, imagine filling your entire body with air, expanding your lungs and your rib cage and letting your belly be soft and round. With each exhale, imagine you can breathe through the bottoms of your feet and send your breath straight into the ground below you (I know you can't, but the point is to get grounded and present—trust me, it works!).

Step 4: Once you are more present, grounded, and in your body, look at the three columns and begin freewriting. In Column One, write down whatever words come to mind when you read "Wild Dreams and Desires." In Column Two, gently inquire about your why. The point is to discover if your dreams and desires are really yours *or* if other people's expectations or cultural norms are influencing them. For example, if I wrote "A cabin in the woods" in Column One, I might write "Because I love to be immersed in nature" in Column Two. Finally, in Column Three, write down what feels real for you after examining what you revealed in Column Two. My example: The thought of living in a cabin, waking up with the sounds of nature, taking long walks down wooded paths, and breathing in the fresh air every day feels exactly right in my body. I feel relaxed and happy when I picture this scene of me in my cabin home.

I realized after doing a version of this exercise during one of Elizabeth's weekend workshops that it has never been my true desire to be thin or what's conventionally considered fit. I love my body just as she is, which happens to be a little soft and a lot curvy. The realization occurred when, in relation to a supposed dream of a slim, muscular body, I looked at my "Really, Why?" and saw that none of the reasons I listed were mine. They were all expectations and desires belonging to other people. That moment marked the beginning of a new phase of my relationship with my body, one marked by surrender, grace, and forgiveness. I'm no longer longing for a body I don't have. Instead, I'm enjoying the process of getting to know and love the body I live in more deeply.

Move through this exercise yourself and see how the steps feel to you. And just like all the exercises in this book, adjust the process as necessary to make the practice your own. There are no strict guidelines, no hard-and-fast rules for you to follow. Part of creating a practice that works for you is experimentation. Keep what works and throw out the rest. What you'll be left with will be a perfect formula for your success.

Release the Idea that It All Has to Be Done Right Now (or at All, or by You)

This is the fun part, where I get to share exactly how I manage my busy-mom-life schedule. These three self-care scheduling tools serve as energetic life preservers, rescuing me from overwhelm and my tendency to overstretch my time and energetic and physical capacities.

You might remember the words that the incomparable Chaka Khan sang in her 1978 hit "I'm Every Woman." She proclaimed herself to be like all women, able to handle anything that needed to be done easily and naturally. I have no doubt that everything she sang was true, but it's also true that managing my mess hardly feels natural most days. It takes a lot of practice and a ton of grace.

Ms. Khan made a powerful statement, but you can see how the attitude of "I got this. I got *all* of this" can get us women into trouble. Or we might just need to approach her statement with a little bit of nuance. To make her message work for you, you might need to squeeze in an extra line, maybe something like "Because I know how to delegate responsibilities to other people, ask for help, and schedule my calendar with grace and self-care to preserve my sanity."

Yes, we all have the same 24 hours in a day as Beyoncé, but saying that isn't to shame anyone. To get where Beyoncé is, she had to make a lot of choices in her life. She operates at an extraordinary level, and that requires a high level of discernment about what she will and won't make part of her schedule or allow to take up space in her head. So, while you might not have a celebrity bank account or support staff (I sure don't), you do have the option to say yes or no, to ask for help, and to prioritize your to-do list. You also have the choice to extend yourself grace and forgiveness when you drop the ball. Your days belong to you, and even though you are responsible for so much, it's up to you to decide what gets your valuable attention. The good news is that you're already like Beyoncé. Reading this book is a way of asking for help while empowering yourself at the same time. I'm here and ready to support you, and you're about to make your motherload feel so much lighter.

Now that we've talked a lot about release, it's time to organize what actually belongs to you (so you can let go of controlling the rest). Yes, I know, that's still a lot. I got you covered in the next chapter with my top three tools for managing my schedule and my sanity.

CHAPTER 9

CREATING A SCHEDULE THAT WORKS FOR YOU

I wrote the subtitle for this book based on the three things I most crave in motherhood: ease, space, and grace. For a long time I thought I would need a magical potion (and probably a few good spells) to make that happen. But what I realized was that making motherhood easier, roomier, and way more graceful isn't a magical process at all; it really just comes down to timing. It's hard to find ease, space, and grace when you're spinning 60 plates (and you actually care if one of them breaks).

But as I hope you've begun to see, we don't have to spin all 60—and who cares if a few break, anyway? We can always ask someone else in the house to sweep it up. Managing the motherload is all about creating a practice that gives us the time, emotional energy, and physical freedom to just breathe. But sometimes breathing demands that we better schedule our breaths, and find the time to breathe even when we're standing in a kitchen filled with broken plates.

"I see all these moms who can do everything, and I think, 'I should really have them do some stuff for me.'"

— Unknown

Tool #1: How to Practice Self-Care When You Don't Have Time to Shower

Grace—self-love, self-forgiveness, and surrendering to what is—practiced through sensible self-care is nonnegotiable for me, and I want you to feel the same. Don't worry, I'm not going to propose that you make time for expensive weekend retreats or hourlong bubble baths (but please indulge if that's your thing). I want to offer the idea that self-care is sometimes *not* taking the bath. It's knowing that after you've finished a really long day of dealing with super-difficult short people, the last pressure you need to put on yourself is making time for a shower. Self-care is simply whatever feels good for you in the moment and helps to repair and prepare you for the next moment. Because returning to mom life isn't optional.

My self-care looks like a lot of things, and it always fits into my schedule. You might not identify with everything on my list as self-care. I didn't always see each item that way, either. Redefining what self-care means for me helped me to recognize and appreciate all the ways I can care for myself more easily every day. But I realized that when I look at normal, everyday activities that bring me happiness as "self-care," I can more easily access happiness. This reframing was also critical to my emotional healing. Like I mentioned before, being grateful for the little things can help so much.

Here's a list of cheap, easy, and schedule-friendly self-care practices I treat myself to often:

- Practicing short meditations or repeating affirmations to myself
- Journaling
- Organizing my personal spaces (my work desk, closet, or studio)
- Talking on the phone with a friend
- Listening to an audiobook during my *definitely-not-daily* shower (my waterproof Bluetooth shower speaker is my favorite thing in the Universe right now)
- Running errands by myself
- Decorating my Passion Planner (my favorite paper planner)
- Eating chocolate-covered espresso beans alone in my laundry room because I'm not sharing them with anyone!
- Saying no

Use mine, make your own, or mix it up however you'd like. Your self-care practices are yours to create, enjoy, and modify over time. It's also fun to pick a theme for your self-care routine. One of my favorite themes is learning. I take workshops whenever I can on topics ranging from social justice to stained-glass making, but my self-care learning practice is usually something like listening to an audiobook. Freedom is another theme. I welcome anything that brings with it a sense of freedom. Start creating your self-care routine right now by picking a theme (a term that represents how you want to feel or what you want to experience through acts of self-care) and develop a short list of activities that support that theme. Jot them down here:

Your Theme Word: _____

_____

Your Self-Care Activities: _____

_____

1. _____

_____

2. _____

_____

3. _____

_____

Tool #2: How to Say "No" Guilt-Free (Even to Kids)

The one action that has freed me from an oppressive schedule more than any other is saying no. My four-year-old, Annie, and I have a little ritual. About once every other day, she asks me if I want to play a game with her. I usually say yes right away or give her a time when I'll be available, which is almost always within an hour. Half the time, it goes downhill from there—downhill and off a cliff. Annie's favorite game is a princess version of Go Fish that is possibly the longest and most boring children's game I've ever endured. So, I counter her offer with a list of games we regularly enjoy playing together, sometimes also suggesting something new. I don't know what her obsession with Disney Princess Go Fish is about, but it sends her straight off a ledge when I decline the request to play it with her.

I don't like playing Princess Go Fish, but I *do* like playing with Annie. And that's exactly how I explain my position to her. I tell her that playing games is fun when both participants *want* to do it, not when we *have* to do it, so it should be a game we both enjoy. I explain that as soon as we can find a game we both like, we can play. She calms down within a minute or two (or a few more than that if she's overdue for a nap), and we move on with a round of Dr. Seuss Matching Game or Candy Land.

This is a very simple example of how I treat every task on my schedule and how I honor my Grand Vision of who I want to be and how I want to show up in this world. If I'm in wild, soulful, truthful expression, I'm not going to suffer through a game that makes my brain explode. I'm going to say no and opt for something that feels good instead.

This interaction with Annie serves a dual purpose. It reminds her of how much I really, *really* hate playing Princess Go Fish, and it teaches her how to say no with confidence, honesty, and tact. What I want for all of my children—but especially for my daughters—is for them to grow up feeling empowered to say no when they don't want to do something and "Hell, yes!" when they do. "Annie, you know I don't like Princess Go Fish, but I have so much fun playing with you. Let's pick out a game we both like." Her response isn't always pleasant, but it's getting better all the time. Four-year-olds need a lot of grace in the "shifting moods" department. And then there are times when I can't resist her big brown eyes and sweet little smile, and I suffer through a game of Princess Go Fish with my favorite little princess because it means that much to her.

When we offer truthful explanations delivered with tact and compassion, we are creating the perfect recipe for positive interaction. I no longer use methods like "because I said so" or avoidance or lying. I used to lie to my kids dozens of times every day just to avoid conflict or a time-consuming back-and-forth: "No, the ice-cream truck plays music when it's *out* of ice cream." Now, I know it's possible to be honest *and* compassionate in every circumstance. And it teaches my kids to honor their own feelings, boundaries, and integrity. "Today isn't an ice-cream truck day, but I promise to pick some up the next time I go to the store." And then I keep my promise. (Honest communication is such a juicy topic that we're going to dive deeper into in Chapter 12!)

How I negotiate Annie's game requests is scalable to any situation. The formula is basically the same no matter what task I'm considering, and it's something that can work for you, too. All I do is ask myself a quick series of questions after imagining first saying yes and then no and examining how each answer feels in my body. I've been doing this for years, so the inner Q&A session happens almost instantaneously.

- Do I want to do the thing?
- Does it fit into who I want to be and how I want to show up in this world?
- Can I communicate my response in a kind and honest way?

If I answer yes to any of those questions, I usually just go ahead and do it (or get help getting it done). But if I answer no to even one of them or if my yes feels a little uncertain, I dig a little deeper with a few more questions. Am I answering from a place of inner wisdom? Or from a fear of missing out? Do I want to do the task only out of guilt? Or because of misplaced feelings of obligation? Or is it something that feels vital to my life and relationships?

And then I look at how it fits into my Grand Vision. Am I motivated to do it because it supports who I want to be and how I want to show up? Or am I just comparing myself to other moms on Instagram and thinking that it's something they would do? What would the future me say to this task or opportunity (and that includes playing a round of Princess Go Fish)? What would future me do (or #WWFMD)?

And finally, if I do have to say no, I think about how best to communicate my reply. How can I do it in a way that honors both my truth and the person I need to say no to—including my little brown-eyed princess?

My day is a garden, just like my life. I plant seeds for what I want to accomplish, and the wind (the random nature of mom life) carries the seeds of wildflowers and weeds. I plant things like paying bills on Mondays and Kiddie Yoga on Wednesdays. Princess Go Fish is a weed. Playing with Annie is a wildflower. I decide what goes and what stays. It's up to me to make my garden beautiful and sustainable. My schedule is mine to own. You might be thinking, "What about the seasons when a lot has to be planted all at once and the wind is dropping seeds all over the place? How can we be busy and overwhelmed and still be a good mom?"

Recalling my days as a young, broke, overwhelmed single mom of three little kids, I can say this—your perception isn't necessarily your kid's reality. I remember days when I would be in a miserable heap, crying because I didn't know how I was going to pay the electric bill or because my ex was being a world-class asshole. I would make popcorn for dinner, put on a terrible kid's movie about a dog or a pig or whatever, and pretend we were having a party. The kids had a great time, and I got to rest (a reminder that, much like the old couch, my perspective on success can be wildly different from my children's).

Do your best; this time will pass. Your kids love you and think you're great. Their needs are simple. Lean into that. When you're feeling overwhelmed by too many demands and there's not enough of you to go around, revisit the questions I listed before: Do I want to do the thing? Does it fit into who I want to be and how I want to show up in this world? Can I communicate my response in a kind and honest way? Because sometimes, the best answer of all is that it's just time to have some frozen pizza and ice cream for dinner, skip a shower or two, and break out the dry shampoo instead. From there, it's time to advance to Tool #3.

Tool #3: How to Lighten the Motherload with Rocks (in Three Parts)

Managing the motherload can't be approached with rigidity. A mother's schedule has to allow for a good amount of the un-expected, which can create a lot of anxiety for some. I have to manage my obstructions to keep vitality flowing (remember the formula: Vitality = Pressure – Obstruction). I try to be as flexible as possible in both my energetic and physical bodies, as well as in my schedule. Extending grace to myself is one way I create flexibility and flow. Rigidity says that I'm the only one who can do it right and that everything has to be done right now. Grace says there are many ways to get something done and that dead-lines shouldn't be dictated by impatience, ego, or anxiety.

Grace says, "Ask for help." Grace says, "Good enough is perfectly fine." Grace tells me that being a mom is a big, important job, and that I deserve my own love and approval even on the days when I feel like I'm falling short. When I practice grace regularly, my schedule lightens and time expands. Let me show you how to experience a little of the same.

"Be formless, shapeless, like water. When you put water into a cup, it becomes the cup. You put water into a bottle, it becomes the bottle. Put it in a teapot, it becomes the teapot. Water can flow, and it can crash. Be water, my friend."

— Bruce Lee

PART 1: BE THE FLOW YOU WISH TO FEEL

Prepare yourself, at the start of every day or before what you anticipate will be a stressful event, by doing a short physical practice that softens both your energetic and your physical body. I actually use this technique when I feel my anxiety level starting to rise. I imagine my body and breath as water, flowing and moving with ease, adaptable to any container.

Do a quick body scan and notice where you might be holding on to any stress and mindfully release that tension with a big exhale. Notice the muscles behind your eyes (are you squinting?), your jaw (I tend to clench mine when I'm nervous), your shoulders (let them drop away from your ears), your hands (allow them to open like starfish), and your belly. I can't tell you how many women, especially moms who are self-conscious about their midsections, are constantly holding in their bellies. Let your belly be soft. Let it expand and become round on your inhale. And let it return to its natural, easy shape on your exhale.

I used to hold my breath a lot, and I still catch myself doing it sometimes. If you're feeling stressed out or overwhelmed, check your breathing. Spend just a minute or two following your natural inhales and exhales. Let your breath flow in and out, in and out, and notice how just breathing can start to bring you back to center. Inhale through your nose, and exhale through your mouth, with your jaw loose and open.

Use this affirmation to remind yourself to go easy and be the flow you wish to feel: *I am moving through this moment, this day, and my whole life with ease.* And when finding inner flow is difficult, throw on a flowy shirt instead. It's infinitely easier to walk around with a fluffy belly when you're sporting an oversized tee with a sassy message on the front. My favorite says IT'S ONLY CHAOS, and it looks adorable with a pair of easy-breezy leggings and glitter-gold high-tops (because glitter makes everything better).

PART 2: TORCH YOUR TO-DO LIST

I had a friend who would keep a giant to-do list in a spreadsheet. Every morning, she would scan this gargantuan, color-coded list and decide which tasks she would tackle that day. Just thinking about it now causes my chest to tighten a little. I stopped writing general to-do lists ages ago, and I never went back. I still keep a few lists because back-to-school supplies, groceries, and my children's classmates' food allergies are still very real and important things in my life, but I don't keep a giant list of tasks anymore. I'm done with anything that feels overwhelming (when I have a say in the matter, anyway).

My tasks and I connect on a need-to-know basis. Instead of writing everything that needs to be done on one list, I assign each task to a day on my calendar. This practice goes back to the question "Is this something that has to be done right now?" The answer is usually no. So, I figure out when the task *does* have to be done, and I pencil it in on an appropriate date in the future. That's all it takes to never again have to look at a long list of everything you haven't done.

PART 3: PEBBLES, ROCKS, AND BOULDERS

My planner is the single most important physical tool I use to manage my busy life. Technology is awesome, but I can't keep track on an electronic calendar. I need to be able to hold something in my hands, so I've been using paper planners since high school. I also prefer hard copies of books over e-books, and I carry a special notebook to every workshop—paper is my jam. But you can use the method I'm going to teach you with both electronic and paper planners. Do what works for you!

I want my schedule to inspire flexibility, freedom, and flow, so I'm very careful about what I commit to and how I place tasks on my calendar. I hope you are now willing to assign tasks to dates rather than putting them all together on a to-do list. Next, I want to show how I decide which tasks, appointments, and events go on which days.

Picture a stream flowing along a forest floor. The stream is your day. The small sticks or leaves being carried downstream are the random things that happen during your day, like a call from the school that your kid is sick. With several kids in school, I swear it seems like the phone rings every day to alert me that one of them left homework, lunch, or a musical instrument at home. Finally, I imagine the big stuff on my list as boulders—these are the tasks, appointments, and events that require a lot of mental, emotional, or physical energy. If you take a giant boulder and stick it in the middle of the stream, the water has to go around it, but it's still flowing fine. However, if you toss a bunch of big ol' boulders in, you create a dam and nothing is getting by. The water will keep splashing up against the rocks and dropping all the crap it was carrying right there in a great big pile. Obstruction has completely stopped your flow.

I've had more great-big-pile-of-crap days than I like to admit. Some were unavoidable. Sometimes, a lot of big stuff outside of my control happened all at once. But most of the time, the drama was self-inflicted. I tried to shove too much into one day because I believed everything was up to me, or I was taking on opportunities just because they sounded good, or I was trying to keep up with the perfect Kiddie Yoga mom who showed up to the last class with a fresh blowout and homemade unicorn cupcakes. Today, if I need cupcakes for a party, I just pay Kiddie Yoga mom to make them for me, or I run by Dunkin' Donuts on the way. My kids' friends happen to love that I send donuts to every party.

How I Organize My Calendar

- Only one boulder, an energetically taxing event like a speaking engagement or *another* conference with my teenager's physics teacher, is allowed per day (if I can help it). If it's a ginormous boulder, I might skip a day or two before I book another one.

- Rocks and pebbles (minor tasks like phone calls, errands, and other everyday obligations) get scattered here and there on the dates when they actually need to be done. I've gone to bed too many nights feeling like a failure because I didn't get *all* the things done, even when most of those things didn't even *need* to get done. When your schedule is packed with a ton of tasks that aren't priorities, you're setting yourself up for disaster. Your only options are to hustle in spite of your well-being or feel like crap because you didn't finish what you set out to do. Toss the rocks and pebbles where they belong instead of letting them collect in a big pile that blocks your healthy flow.

- Nothing out of alignment with my Grand Vision gets a yes from me, ever. That doesn't mean I never do things that are a drag. Big parts of my Grand Vision require a certain level of financial success and kids who have actually moved out of my house, so tasks that support either of those always make it onto the schedule. That might mean working late and missing one of my kid's sports games or saying no to an important networking event to drive my daughter back to college. It's easy to decide. Just ask, "What would future me do?"

- Empty space is a valuable thing, and I honor it. I'm no longer interested in being busy for the sake of being busy. I'm not impressed by women who run themselves into the ground trying to achieve perfection. My family looks like a gaggle of circus monkeys on Instagram because I just don't have time for staged photoshoots, millennial pastel storyboards, and matching outfits. I use the spare minutes I manage to collect throughout the day to meditate in parking lots between errands. My mental health is a priority. At this stage of my mom game, I just want to know that my kids are okay, that my best is good enough, and that the struggle doesn't always have to be real. I want to be happy at the end of my day, knowing that the exhaustion is worth it and I'm doing life (mostly) well.

In the end, the biggest parts of creating a schedule that serves me are staying connected to my Grand Vision and understanding that almost no task is life or death and that grace is the most beautiful (and useful) gift I can give myself every day. I'm a strong, resilient, competent, successful mother who regularly asks for help, drops the ball on really important stuff, and places daily showers really low on my list of priorities. I even let my four-year-old fold towels the other day. And the world didn't end (as far as I can tell).

Meditation for Abundance

PREPARATION FOR YOUR MEDITATION

I used to resist the whole concept of "manifesting abundance" because it felt icky. I'm not motivated by making lots of money or hoarding wealth. It's more important to me to be able to share what I have with others. There's a flaw in that, though. How can I give something away without having more than I need? Now, I call in and welcome abundance of all kinds—financial abundance, abundant love, and whatever opportunities will help me to be and do more in this world. Success requires more than enough. It's a whole lot of what's good. That's exactly what I want for myself, and for you, too.

POSITION / BREATH / GAZE

Let's try something different for this meditation. I want you to feel joyful in your posture, so sit up nice and tall with your chest open and your face shining forward. Now, try smiling just a little. I'm not talking about a big, goofy grin that will hurt after a minute. Smile like you would if you were thinking of a happy memory, savoring the moment all by yourself. Practice Even Breath for this meditation, the technique where you match the length of your exhales to that of your inhales (see page 51). Like always, it's up to you whether you close your eyes or keep them open—choose whatever feels most comfortable.

WORDS FOR YOUR PRACTICE

The following message is meant to be read out loud and with a smile on your face. Your thoughts are powerful, but speaking your thoughts out loud gives them life. Adding the energy of a smile infuses joy. This meditation (and the rest of the meditations in this book) will be different from the previous two because both your message and your mantra will be offered in the first person. I want you to get used to boldly declaring positive statements about yourself and your life. Read slowly and with reverence. Know that as you read, you are already beginning to embody what is written.

Abundant love. Abundant joy. Abundant energy. Abundant time. I call on abundant blessings. I am worthy of all that I have and more.

I offer my love. I offer my joy. I offer my energy. I offer my time. I feel blessed to share my gifts with the world.

I am a worthy steward for the abundant love and blessings of the Universe. I am grateful for all that I am, all that I've been given, and all that I have to share. What blesses me moves through me and blesses others. I am a vessel for infinite blessings because I give freely and with a loving heart. I am worthy of having big dreams and seeing them come true because my success serves everyone I love.

YOUR MANTRA

Return your focus to your Even Breath. You're smiling again because you know blessings are on the way! Read your mantra below and commit it to memory. Repeat it on every exhale for as long as it feels good. Remember to pause after every repetition at the bottom of your exhale to smile and feel the power of the mantra. And when you're ready, take one last big breath, smile big, and return to your day.

I am worthy of abundant blessings.
I welcome them with joy.

Phase 4

NURTURE
AND GROW

CHAPTER 10

HEALTHY ROOTS

"Can't you see it? Can't you see that he's you and that you're Mom?" I heard my younger sister's words, but I was struggling to process them. "This is exactly what happened with you and Mom. He's acting just like you, and you're reacting just like she did. You have to see it, don't you?" She was talking about my oldest son and the conflict that was escalating between us. He was already living away from home, and I was desperate for answers on how to fix what was happening. It took a few moments for her words to land, but when they did, it was like a fog had lifted. She was right. The war between my son and me was just a replay of a 20-year-old story, a scenario I had lived before, just with different players. I couldn't believe I hadn't seen it.

It was only a month after my 17th birthday when I made a dramatic exit from my mother's house and went out on my own. Arguments like the one we had that night were commonplace—complete with name-calling and objects being hurled across the room. I remember that we were fighting about my stepfather. She was defending him and calling me a liar. I lost it, and my boyfriend had to drag me out of the house, literally kicking and screaming in a fit of rage and hurt. I remember feeling so betrayed by my mother, and the only way to express that pain was through hysterical outbursts. It was easy for me to see myself in my son's behavior. What I wasn't prepared for was seeing my mother's behavior in myself.

"In search of my mother's garden, I found my own."
— Alice Walker

My sister's words hit me like a ton of bricks. But they also gave me the first glimmer of hope I had felt in a while. It made sense, and I wanted to dig deeper. So, after our conversation, I spent some time in meditation. Meditation is the simplest and most effective way for me to explore difficult feelings, especially when I can't quite sort out exactly what those feelings are.

My meditation session wasn't the first time I'd thought about the night I left my mother's house when I was 17. But this was different. This time I was looking for answers. Up until then, I had used my version of what happened and my hurt feelings to justify my anger toward my mother. And then, after she died, my anger turned to shame. I was filled with regret over the time we had lost. But shame and regret rarely get us to the truth of a matter. And as I would find out 20 years later, they couldn't keep me from repeating the same destructive behavior with my own son.

With a Clear Mind, You Can See Forever

I went into my meditation with the intention of clearing up my confusion and trying to gain a new perspective on what had happened back then. If our negative stories are left unchallenged for too long, they can start to feel like facts, and I had been holding on to mine too tightly for a long time. Those old stories can be dangerous things. They can keep us stuck in bad habits or in conflict with the people we love. My stories about my mother were long overdue for a closer examination.

I created space for this meditation—ample time, no distractions. I said a prayer at the beginning, asking for my heart to be open to whatever truth needed to be revealed. I asked for wisdom to guide me toward anything that would bring me closer to healing my relationship with my son. I closed my eyes and sent my attention to my breath. With each exhale, I released more tension from every part of my body. And when I felt comfortable and relaxed enough, I visualized my way back to my mother's house on that fateful night.

A surge of emotions filled my body. I could feel a tightening in my chest as I used my mind's eye to scan the dining room, the piano, and the candlesticks I would grab and throw across the room. I remembered screaming and wanting to cry. I reminded myself that I was safe in meditation and that none of what was upsetting me was happening anymore. But I also felt something new coming up—frustration. I was screaming the same words over and over again, and my mother was just staring at me. She couldn't hear me—she wasn't listening. I grabbed the candlesticks and threw them. I screamed louder. My boyfriend ran into the house and dragged me outside. It was over.

I took a few slow, deep, grounding breaths and returned to the scene, this time as my mother. I put myself in her body and watched myself through her eyes. The frustration was back, but I was feeling it as her this time. I saw the teenage me screaming, angry and out of control. As my mother, I felt helpless. I wanted to hug me, shake me, soothe me . . . but all I could do was stand there, stunned into paralysis. There was no reaching teenage me in that moment. And then, I saw my son. "Can't you see it? Can't you see that he's you and that you're Mom?" My sister's words landed in my gut again, shattering any illusions I had been clinging to about that night and making me reconsider my history with my mother. Those old stories suddenly felt fresh and new, and I realized that I had gotten a lot of it wrong.

> *"Nothing ever goes away until it has taught us what we need to know."*
> —Pema Chödrön

It's funny that we say to our children when they're misbehaving, "One day, you'll have kids of your own, and I hope they act just like you!" What I used to see as a silly, snarky half threat I now see as a call for understanding and compassion. It's a tall order, though. Can children ever really feel true compassion for their parents while still under their "rule"? Is it possible for anyone to truly understand another person's perspective if they haven't walked in their shoes? They can feel empathy, sure. But true understanding often requires a similar lived experience (particularly for such a unique and complex experience as parenthood). My opinions of my mother were based entirely on her performance in that role. It wasn't until I lost her that I started to understand that she was a woman outside of being my mom. And now I considered for the first time that before she was a mother, she was a girl just like me—in search of acceptance, validation, and love.

My son's rejection of me breaks my heart. I can't sugarcoat it or lie and say that I can accept any part of it. I can't. I grieve for our relationship every single day, and the pain isn't letting up with time. On the contrary, I worry that the divide is only growing deeper and will be more difficult to mend. My feelings have made me realize how my rejection of my mother broke *her* heart. There were wrongs that led up to every argument and period of estrangement, and as the parent, she held most of the responsibility and fault. But none of that means it didn't kill her to think her daughter despised her. I told my mother I hated her more times than I can count, to her face and in innumerable private moments when I cried alone and prayed to God to heal our broken bond. So, I got a kid who is just like I was. The joke's on me! But I don't have to be the mother my mom was. I have a choice to break the cycle, to end the generational pain right now and forever. And I want to show you how to begin to do that, too.

An Early Harvest

Let's take a moment to look at your own journey through this book. First, you planted seeds with loving, wise intention. Then, the Universe added its own untamed magic with weeds and wildflowers. You surveyed your unruly garden and used Divine Discernment again and again. You made it part of your practice. As a result, you have built a solid foundation of gratitude. You respect and appreciate the random and sometimes chaotic wildflower moments. You can even see the big and little blessings as weeds produce flowers and cover your lawn with clover. And those seeds you've planted have cracked open. These fragile but determined seedlings are reaching up through the soil—on the cusp of breaking through the surface. Now, it is the time to nurture.

The nurturing phase calls for action. The growth that happens during this phase requires a lot of love and care. Whether it's a passion project or a child, your inner wisdom and loving attention will be called upon to make growth successful. None of this will happen perfectly. We're looking for progress, not perfection. And progress demands that you extend grace to yourself again and again and again.

Moving forward also requires looking back. Examining your roots can give you powerful insight into current circumstances. I'll guide you through exercises that will help you safely examine your childhood and your relationship with your parents. This was a part of the work I resisted for too long, and it's the part that brought to light the most profound realizations. It made a path for forgiveness and healing that opened me up to better relationships in every area of my life. If you're ready, now's your chance to begin (or to deepen) this powerfully healing work.

So, let's do it! Let's dig. Let's sift through all the layers of dirt to where the answers are buried. Let's examine the roots. Because when a plant is yellowing and droopy, you look to the soil to heal the leaves. That's exactly what we're going to do in the next activity. This is the extra-fun part of the book where you get to find out exactly how much you have in common with your parents, and how what you *don't* have in common may be because of them, too. It's time to get your hands dirty!

The two exercises in this chapter are adapted from work I've done with my life coach and what I frequently offer to my clients and coaching groups. Though I've already done this work in great depth, I revisit it whenever I need to get unstuck on a particular issue or when I'm trying to sort out some confused feelings about a situation. You'll see what I mean as you go through the steps and read my examples. Once again, I'm offering my personal work, raw and unedited, for your reference. It's important to me that you see my process before doing it yourself. Because I truly am a product of this work—and I would never offer anything that I haven't already tested on myself and been convinced that it worked.

This process is going to make you step in front of a mirror—one that reveals it *all*. While that might sound scary, it's actually where the real magic happens. Because that "all" also includes crystal clear insights into what you've been struggling to figure out. It reveals the path to freedom from old stories and bad habits. I'm so excited for you!

Exercise 1: Parent Traits and How They Live in You

The first exercise explores your parents' traits and their influence on you. It's okay if you only had one caregiver present; just do the work for that one. Include stepparents if they played a big role in your life. My own work from the very first time I did this exercise followed these steps. I want to note here that it was years after my mother passed that I first attempted this process. I know everything between my mother and me would have been very different if I'd done this work earlier—we could have healed what was broken in our relationship. But when she was alive, those issues felt insurmountable. I wish I'd known then how simple transformation can be.

Step 1: List the dominant positive and negative traits of each of your parents, describing how each trait showed up in them. You can keep it short and simple here—there's no need to write a book. Just write what first comes to mind. As with all the exercises so far, I recommend keeping your notes in a safe place for future reference or to expand upon later.

Step 2: For each trait, write a short statement about how it lives in you. This doesn't mean you behave in the exact same way as your parent. You might have made great efforts to do and be the opposite of your parent and have a completely different trait as a result of that work. Write about that. Let these examples guide you through your work.

MY FATHER: FRIGHTENED, KIND, WEAK, CREATIVE/TALENTED, LOYAL, SIMPLE

Frightened: He was very insecure and afraid of the world and the opinions of others.
How it lives in me: I have a certain amount of social anxiety that makes me suffer through interactions with people.

Kind: He would give anyone the shirt off his back. He believed and embodied Christian kindness.
How it lives in me: Everything I have, I share. My gifts are gifts from God that belong to the world.

Weak: He never stood up for himself, and people walked all over him.
How it lives in me: I fear looking weak, so I'm aggressive and quick to assert dominance in situations.

Creative/talented: My dad loved to draw and build things in his spare time. He was an artist at heart.
How it lives in me: If I'm not expressing myself creatively, I get bored and restless.

Loyal: He loved his family and gave his whole life to support them.
How it lives in me: I put my husband and kids before myself.

Simple: He only had an eighth-or ninth-grade education and was afraid of rich or educated people.
How it lives in me: I dropped out of high school in my senior year, even though I was a top student. I feel like people judge me because I'm not educated.

MY MOTHER: SMART, INSECURE, SEXUAL, STRONG, CARING

Smart: My mom was good at everything, and she could out-argue anyone.
How it lives in me: I take pride in my intelligence, and I love to debate.

Insecure: She always doubted herself and her talent. She was constantly looking for outside validation (mostly from men). My mom was always eager to please.
How it lives in me: I engage in a lot of self-praise. I never want to appear unsure or insecure. But I do always try to get people to like me.

Sexual: My mother was promiscuous and subservient to men.
How it lives in me: I'm very flirtatious, but I don't like that about myself. I don't want to be objectified.

Strong: She was physically strong and capable. My mom was one of the hardest workers I've ever known, both in her physicality and in her desire for perfection.
How it lives in me: Being strong is important to me. I rarely let men do physical work for me, and I look at other women who do that as weak. I want to know how to do everything. I take care and execute every aspect of my business, from social media to graphic design, community building, and marketing.

Caring: My mother took care of people—even better than she cared for her children. Her friends all looked at her as an amazing and compassionate caregiver.
How it lives in me: I want all my friends and family to feel protected by me, like I have their backs. I always step in and take care of the kinds of things everyone else avoids. However, I shy away from affection with my kids.

"Thou shalt not judge, because thou hast f*cked up in the past also."
—— Unknown

Doing this exercise did a couple of things for me. It forced me to sit with opinions I had never explored. Many of the traits I listed were picked because they affected me in a negative way. It wasn't easy for me to say good things about my parents. At the time when I first did this exercise, I was doing it because I was hurting and seeking to rid myself of that pain. My parents were gone, and I missed them so much, but I hadn't worked through all the anger and resentment I felt toward them (as you can probably see in my answers). I was still blaming them for a lot of what was wrong in my life. But I began to realize those resentments were only evidence that I had a lot of work left to do. Exploring each trait, even with just a few words, made me see that my parents' actions weren't all about me. I was the center of *my* universe, but not *theirs*. They were human beings outside of being my mom and dad, and in describing their traits, I revealed their pains, not just mine. And in honoring their pain, I revealed a compassion in myself that I hadn't felt before. Eventually, that compassion would lead to forgiveness.

Forgiveness becomes infinitely easier when the so-called bad guy looks, sounds, and acts a lot like you. It had always been easy for me to make my parents out as "bad," but it wasn't so easy after seeing how their traits now showed up in me—how I *chose* to behave just like them. I've done so much work on myself. It would be easy for me to say, "I'm done. I'm healed. I'm enough. I can stop working on myself now. I can stop trying to be better."

But that's probably not the case for 99 percent of the people on the planet. We are always learning, and the truth is that I still have a lot of work to do. The fractured relationship with my son couldn't be stronger evidence of that truth. I had to go digging to figure out why I am the way I am. I had to forgive myself to feel worthy of healing. I am not a hopeless cause. But if I'm forgiving myself for the same traits and actions that I saw in my parents, I had to extend that forgiveness to them, too. And that's how to begin taking generational pain, a legacy of heartache, and start the healing process. Every generation that comes after me will benefit from my forgiving my parents.

The truth is, most of us still harbor some resentments over our childhoods. Whether the trespasses were great or small, it's not hard to think that previous generations could have done things differently, if not better. But no matter the traumas, the pain we carry about those histories often rivals the pain of the experience itself. Now, I recognize that some people's childhoods resembled a horror movie, and forgiveness can be tougher for some than others. But in clearing out the pain of our pasts, we make room for more joy today, even when the events are more recent.

I used another version of this work to sort out feelings I was having about the son I'm in conflict with and his two siblings who share the same father, my ex-husband. The unstable and sometimes volatile relationship I have with my ex only adds stress to my interactions with the children we share. I'm constantly afraid of pushing them away, and I blame myself for not giving them the family they deserve. Our bond can feel tenuous, and my fear of it breaking can bring out the worst in me. So this time, instead of listing my parents' traits, I listed my ex-husband's and mine. And then, I wrote how they show up in each of my children. It was incredibly healing to list all the wonderful things their father has given to them—their athleticism, musical talent, and love of math, among many other things.

This version of the exercise was much harder and took a bigger emotional toll on me. More forgiveness was needed to get through it. I had to forgive the person I was when I chose my ex, and I had to forgive him, too. He gave me three wonderful children who reflect a lot of who he was and still is, and I can't hate him and love them fully. Sure, I hate a lot of what he's done, but I forgive him for the sake of our children. This part of my journey is one that's still ongoing, so I'll leave it here.

DOWN TO THE ROOT

We live in a world of messaging. From traditional to social media, to cultural expectations and the side-eye from strangers, we are bombarded by opinions on how we should think and feel and what we should do. But even beyond the world around us, most of us are still guided by the messaging we received in childhood. We tell ourselves things all the time without reflecting on where those ideas come from.

Remember in Chapter 1 when we learned how to talk back to our inner voices? Well, now we're going to combine that with a little parent work. Are you ready to get to the root of your own negative messaging? It isn't always fun (kind of like a root canal), but when we realize that the negative thoughts and perspectives aren't really true reflections of who we are, but rather distorted images from our past, we can be relieved of them. And what joy it is to be relieved of pain.

Exercise 2: Beyond the Talkback

Instead of just writing the negative message and how you talked back to it (like we did on page 14), I want you to expand on each by adding a third step to the practice. Ask yourself the question "Where does this come from?" Chances are this will bring up more stuff about your parents. Here's how I've used this practice in a present-day area in my life—my business, a place where I sometimes still struggle to be confident.

STEP 1: MY NEGATIVE MESSAGE

"You don't have what it takes to make it to the top." This negative self-talk is often triggered by seeing someone in my space/industry who is performing at a high level. I feel jealous and defeated, and then I feel ashamed of those feelings. I tell myself that I'll never have the know-how, connections, look, clothes, money, education, or sophistication to be accepted in the circles that will allow me to succeed on a big scale. I immediately recall times during my childhood when I felt most out of place or conspicuously poor. I feel that same shame and embarrassment, and then I tell myself that this is just who I am, and things will never be any different.

STEP 2: MY TALKBACK

"This is a fantasy you have created that doesn't look at all like the reality of what you've experienced. You have been accepted and celebrated in every circle you've entered. People you respect come to you for advice and constantly offer their help. The people you want to serve already follow you, buy your products, and seek your expertise. You are constantly getting opportunities your peers wish they had. No matter how you feel inside, you always present yourself in a professional, put-together way. People like you and like being around you. And before you go on the Internet and look at what other people are doing, you wake up feeling good about yourself and your life. You have accomplished everything in your life despite not having had a lot of the things people think you need to get where you are. You succeed every day and support yourself and your family with this work. You are honest, dedicated, hardworking, funny, and smart. You don't have to belong in a circle. You create the circle. You build the community. You can choose to be the leader. Step into that choice."

STEP 3: WHERE DOES THIS COME FROM?

My father had severe social anxiety, the type that kept him at home for most of his life except when he went to work or church. He always said he felt judged for his clothes or the way he looked (he had bad teeth). I had to buy him clothes to wear to my wedding because he complained that he didn't have anything to wear and couldn't afford it. He never went to any of my school events, including my art shows or my graduations. He never met any of my teachers.

My mother was always very beautiful, put-together, outgoing, and well-liked. She had a striking appearance, a very flashy and over-the-top bohemian look. She liked the attention, which made me feel super self-conscious when I was younger. Getting too much attention makes me feel objectified.

EMERGING FROM THE DARKNESS

This exercise didn't make all my issues disappear, but it did shine a light on an old negative story. And sometimes that's all it takes to diminish the power of something that's been holding you back—to reveal how insignificant it really is.

Your negative message is not who you are. Period. And it only has as much power as you choose to give it. As you take away its power in the present moment, you take away its energy to return in the future. You don't have to fix anything. Don't put that pressure on yourself. Sometimes we shine the light, expose what's *really* going on, and are able to let that old negative energy turn to dust in the wind. And the other times, we just have to accept the pain.

We have to remove the obstacles in order to experience more vitality, and there is nothing more formidable than the emotional ones we just don't know how to clear.

I'm still at what's probably the beginning of a very long journey of healing with my son. Some problems aren't so easily solved. Some obstacles take more time to find a way around. And we have to learn to live with and be okay with those parts of the healing process, too.

"Deep in their roots, all flowers keep the light."
— Theodore Roethke

After it's all done, remember to forgive yourself for your very natural reactions to circumstances you hadn't quite figured out yet. Know that it was all part of the process of growing and discovering. Every moment leading up to now has been exactly what was needed to get you here—good and bad. It all mattered. With that knowledge, you'll be able to nurture future growth with more awareness and compassion. You are able to surrender to the past in order to create the future you deserve. When you understand where you came from and *why* things are, you can move through life with more grace, power, and ease than ever before.

CHAPTER 11

GROWING YOUR HIGHER SELF

I've shared what I *do* to manage my motherload, but I haven't shared much about how I *keep doing* it—how I stay motivated and dedicated to my personal growth. Sure, I love my kids, but that motivates me to keep *them* well loved and fed. Me? Not so much. It's easy for me to root for my children's hopes and dreams, but going after my own requires a certain amount of self-love that I had to nurture over time.

Nurturing takes work, whether it's nurturing ourselves, nurturing our dreams, or nurturing our children. All of these take time, belief, willingness, and commitment to the process. They also take support, which a lot of women find is in short supply. But believe me, there is a force that is always there for you to call on for help.

"You have a direct connection with God that no man, minister, or teacher can come between. When you talk, He listens." I remember being just five years old when my mother shared that bit of wisdom with me for the first time. I've always been a person who imagines every message as a picture, so I immediately saw a red string traveling from my heart straight into Heaven. It was like the string that connected two plastic cups to make a pretend telephone.

Believing that God was always there for me created a sense of confidence and courage that is always present beneath the surface. Although that part of my root got buried by a lot of dirt over time, I'm lucky to have been given a foundational sense of being supported that I can still settle into when the weight of my problems feels too heavy. Down deep, I've always known I was loved by something very powerful, and that has inspired a sense of duty to love myself. My life is a gift, and I work hard not to be an ungrateful recipient. There's a force that's pulling for me, one that I'm connected to at all times, that is ready and willing to listen to my hopes, dreams, and prayers. That force wants me to be a huge success.

You don't have to believe in God or a higher power to feel supported by a loving force. Your higher self is powerful in her own right, and the work you're doing in this book will help you connect with her and feel held by her strength. I promise that moving toward your goals can feel really good when you know you're supported and you have the right tools for doing the work.

I want every woman who reads this book to feel like she's entitled to having big dreams *and* seeing them come true, regardless of her circumstances. You can go after what you want, strive for success, love yourself, and still be the mother you believe your children deserve. You can and will do it, because you're never on your own. I promise.

The Meaning of Success

Let's start by defining success, a version of success that works for you. You have your Grand Vision, but that's what's waiting for you in the future. Waiting to feel successful until you've checked off all the boxes on your "my most amazing life" list isn't ideal because it probably won't keep you motivated. Think about it. If success can't be enjoyed until you hit your goal weight, or your business makes its first [insert only-in-my-wildest-dreams dollar amount here], or your kid goes off to college, what the heck do you call every moment leading up to all that?

Success isn't necessarily the finish line of getting the thing done. My dreams and my version of success honor the season of life in which I find myself. They honor my desires and my Grand Vision as well as the circumstances of my right now. There have been long stretches of time when I felt fulfilled by just being in the role of mother. Yeah, being *just* a mom is a completely okay thing. It's an amazing thing, really, if that's what you want. In those times, showing up for my babies was all the action I required of myself because I knew there would be a time when I could work on my other dreams. I've had a book in me from the time I was a little girl, but I was patient in the doing. I didn't start my first book until my fifth baby was kicking in my belly. I held the dream close to my heart, never giving it up, knowing that taking action would happen when the season for doing arrived.

Author Joyce Meyer said, "Patience is not simply the ability to wait. It's how we behave while we're waiting." When you're a mother with big dreams, it can feel so hard to be patient. It can be downright scary if you think you might not have the opportunity to work on your own plans. Letting myself dream about the future without pressuring myself to make it happen right away is what allowed me to eventually make my dreams come true. I spent the time when I was not working on my dream creating a life that would support me when I was ready to take action. I talked about my dreams with family and friends, I jotted down ideas in journals, and—most important—I held space for the belief that it would happen when I was ready. Faith, trust, and belief are really hard things to teach, but they're all the key ingredients to making dreams come true. But sometimes, in order to build more faith, trust, and belief, we have to begin to surrender the conviction that those dreams define our success. We have to redefine what success even means.

"Success is liking yourself, liking what you do, and liking how you do it."
— Maya Angelou

What if success isn't a destination but rather a series of tiny wins on the path to your Grand Vision? Wins that are celebrated in the moment. What if you could go to bed every single night feeling successful, even on the days that sucked? Doesn't that sound good? Let me tell you what's going on with me right now. On the day I'm writing this, I'm celebrating the four-old-old wiping her own poopy butt (and remembering to wash her hands—hallelujah!). I took the little kids to Kiddie Yoga, the library, and soccer practice without yelling once. And I unflagged nearly all of my "urgent" emails (mostly by deleting them, but it still counts). I did some good stuff today, and I handled that stuff with grace and humor. Maya Angelou would probably say I rocked this day. Go, me! And even if the most remarkable thing I did today was organize the "watch next" list on my Netflix account, I'm still celebrating me. Because taking time to rest is part of my success plan, too.

See what I did there? In recognizing all the tiny, ordinary, everyday wins, I motivate myself for more. This practice also comforts me when I'm feeling "less than." It reminds me of how every important and precious step toward my Grand Vision is actually just a step toward a life well lived. Over the past few chapters, you declared what you desire most in life in your Grand Vision, you learned how to create a schedule that supports your energetic and physical well-being, and you did some parent work to figure out how you might show up better in motherhood and beyond. You have already accomplished a lot! Now you're ready to start putting all of your new tools to work for you in a way that feels gratifying and joyful.

Jennifer Pastiloff is a mother, author, and yoga teacher who I simply adore. While I followed her online for years, I really fell in love with her work when I read these words: "When I get to the end of my life and I ask one final 'What have I done?' let my answer be 'I have done love.'" Reading those words for the first time felt like being swaddled by a big, comfy blanket, burrito style. I felt held by them. I surrendered to the warmth of her words and took a huge exhale. They felt like truth, like love. They also felt like the definition of success. Living in alignment with my vision every day, in all ways and expressions, is how I measure how successful I am. And if I think hard enough about how that alignment shows up, it's always as love—love for my family, love for my vision, love for myself, and love for this life. Everything is an act of love—from the way I organize my calendar to the way I take care of who and what I love. If I feel like I've "done" love at the end of a day, I am succeeding. And every night before I go to bed, I get to celebrate those wins as if I had just made my biggest dream come true.

Temper Tantrums and Backward Sweatpants

Notice how my definition of success has everything to do with how I show up and nothing to do with things that are happening outside of my control. How many times have you felt like a failure because your kid got a bad grade on a report card or threw a temper tantrum in public? Think back to the last time you went to bed with a pit in your stomach over all the unchecked items on your to-do list (which couldn't have mattered that much because, hey, everyone made it through the day alive and the house didn't burn down, right?). Why not also define success as how you act while you're *moving toward* everything you want instead of just *getting* what you want?

The old me used to take my kids' grades so seriously, and I let their achievements and failures affect my sense of personal value. Now, when one of my kids comes home with less than stellar marks on their report card, I respond with compassion, curiosity, and an even temperament (*most* of the time—when I fail, I catch myself or my kids enthusiastically call me out). But even when my reaction isn't perfect, I try to help them figure out what isn't working in that particular class. From there, we co-create a better plan for going forward. That reaction comes from a place of knowing that I can be a good, successful mother even when my kid is having a hard time at school. If I feel like I'm doing a crappy job as their mom, how can I be confident or effective in helping them? I can't.

The same goes for public temper tantrums. Being a little kid is hard. They want what they want, and they don't understand why they just can't have it when they want it. Imagine how good it would feel after realizing that something has gone terribly wrong with your day, to throw yourself on the floor in the middle of the grocery store and scream at the top of your lungs until someone brings you what you want. I crave that freedom. So, I don't blame a toddler for taking it. And I don't blame myself when my toddler does it. Yes, it can be horrifying when any perceived dirty laundry is put on display for strangers and their judging eyes. That's why whenever I see an exhausted, embarrassed mom trying to wrangle her wild tiny person back into the shopping cart in the housewares aisle at Target, I give her a kind smile that says, "I feel your pain, sister. Stay strong." Then, I help her refold the towels her beautiful child threw all over the floor and place them neatly back on the shelf (just like my mother taught me).

What I also want her to know is that I think she's doing a great job and that I consider her to be a success already. She got herself and her kid dressed and outside. She is successfully surviving this day just like she has survived every day before it. I want her to believe that that's what makes her a good mom and that a screaming toddler doesn't change that fact. I want her to know that believing in herself and her abilities is going to allow her to show up better in every moment—for herself and for her family. She doesn't have to panic when things feel like they're going sideways. Instead, she can confidently say to herself, "I got this. I always have. My success might look different every day, but as long as I'm moving forward, I am succeeding."

You might not feel confident now, but you will. Repeated success fuels confidence. One of my favorite mantras and bits of advice for building confidence is "Do the thing. Don't die. Repeat." That's it. Try the new thing. Live another day. Handle your toddler's temper tantrum or your teenager's disastrous report card like a Buddha. It might feel scary or hard, but you can do that scary, hard thing in the midst of fear or struggle. Do the thing. Surviving it (not dying) is success. Repeat until it's no longer scary, until it's no longer hard. The proof that you can do challenging things will build your confidence. And confidence is like the world's most powerful fertilizer. It will give you the courage to try more new things, to take bigger risks, to make more mistakes, and to forgive and love yourself through it all.

I once did a podcast interview in which I couldn't stop laughing for the first three minutes because I realized I had my pants on backward. I had been wearing them like that all day long without noticing—I was that busy. Ironically, the topic of the interview was how I "have it all" and "keep it together" with five kids and a business. *In backward sweatpants, that's how!* Perfection has not and will never be a requirement for happiness or success. Progress, acceptance, grace, forgiveness, baby steps, and love—those are key characteristics of a happy person's success strategy. The podcast host left the whole laugh-fest in the final version of the show, and I'm so glad she did. I want every mother to know that my days are productive, happy, and *messy*.

Feeling successful, no matter what your days look like, is the first step. The next step is using that feeling to take confident, meaningful action toward your goals. In order to move closer to our goals, we must commit to acting in alignment with our Grand Vision, and that requires accountability. How do I keep myself accountable? With love-centered action.

Crazy, Stupid Love (for Your Vision and Yourself)

We're going to work on relationships in the next chapter, but I want to call on some elements of romantic relationships to help guide the work you're about to do. Take a moment and make a list in your head of what you desire most from a romantic partner—not their qualities, but how you want to be treated by them and how you want to feel when you're with them. We all want to be loved, but what does love look like for you? How does it feel? How does it show up in a relationship? You might wonder why I'm focusing on romantic relationships. Because I want you to imagine the kind of love that lights you up and makes you feel juicy, vibrant, and inspired. Call on the kind of love that makes you do things you normally wouldn't, that makes you take risks, that makes time stop.

The only way I can both go after my dreams and still manage the trials of motherhood is by showing up with big love, both for my Grand Vision and for myself. And let's face it, loving ourselves is ridiculously hard some days. Even in times when I'm pretty cool with myself and wouldn't want to be anyone else, self-love is a weird concept to wrap my head and heart around. On days when loving myself is tricky, I give myself permission to have those mixed emotions. Hating on myself for not loving myself makes no sense, and it's almost like being told to calm down in the middle of an anxiety attack. When has that ever helped anyone?

So, I ask myself, "How do I want a romantic partner to show up for me?" The answer is far easier to access than feelings of self-love. I want their attention, time, and compassion. I want them to speak loving words to and about me. I want to feel turned on and excited about life just by being around them. When I share a wild idea about a big future plan, I want them to light up and say, "That sounds amazing! I think you should go for it!" And when I feel beat up by the day, by the world, by life, I want them to say, "You're doing great. I love you. Is there anything I can do to make this moment easier?"

That's how I call in self-love. I love myself like a lover. I give myself attention, time, and compassion. I recite cheesy feel-good affirmations out loud. I say "YES, YES, YES" to my big (and small, and wacky) ideas. And when I'm feeling like a hot, unshowered mess, I tell myself I'm doing a good job, plop two scoops of vegan Ben & Jerry's into a bowl, and let myself watch four back-to-back episodes of *The Real Housewives of Atlanta* while the kids destroy their playroom. I will clean it one day, but today is not that day.

Because love is the greatest act of surrender. We surrender to the risk that we can and probably will be hurt. We surrender our privacy and lives and yes, sometimes even a few wants and needs for it. And we have to surrender on a lot of hills in order to keep the platoon moving.

Loving ourselves demands the same action. We can't place conditions on self-love, just as we can't set conditions on the love we have for our children. It is simply there—like the wind and the rain and, on good days, which are most days, really, the sun.

Just another note about love here: I don't buy into the concept of having to love yourself in order to be loved. I've lived through too many phases of my life when I hated myself only to have the love of others save my life. Even now, when my *love* for myself is pretty constant, self-*like* comes and goes. So, I play the role of an adoring lover, and I use that perspective to give myself the love I know I deserve (or that I at least want to feel).

Create Your Own Affirmations for Self-Love

When self-love isn't happening on its own, I use mantras to remind myself of how I want to feel and of the important work I have to do to stay on track with my Grand Vision. It's so easy to create your own affirmations for self-love, and the work you've already done is going to help you get started. Your "and" statements from Chapter 6 are the perfect jumping-off point because they're the counter statements to whatever "bad" stuff you have going on in the moment, and they're written in the present tense. Recall the examples I gave you. I've underlined the parts you could use as starter affirmations:

- My bills are stacking up, *and* <u>I have a warm bed to sleep in tonight</u>.
- I sabotaged my healthy eating with all that junk last night, *and* <u>I can choose my next meal with love</u>.
- Everyone is putting all their problems on me, *and* <u>I have the power to set strong boundaries</u>.

As far as self-love affirmations go, these are pretty uninspiring. For an affirmation to do its job, it should be positive and worded in the present tense ("you deserve to feel loved now"), and maybe feel a little uncomfortable to say it. Try something big and bold like "I've gained weight since having the baby, *and* I'm a sensual woman with a beautiful body that I love to touch and to have touched." Loving yourself can feel strange and radical. Let it happen! If your affirmation feels a little silly or self-indulgent, good! The more you say it, the more natural it will feel. Hopefully, over time, you'll be able to proclaim it with ease and even start to believe it. Let me walk you through the process step-by-step and with the specific intention of overcoming a current obstacle.

Step 1: Recall what you want. Go back to your Grand Vision for this one. You already have the blueprint for exactly how you want your life to be, so it makes sense to use it here. Pull desire statements from what you wrote in your Grand Vision. Here's mine: "I want to live in wild, creative expression in my personal and work lives."

Step 2: Name an obstacle that's in your way. This can be a physical obstacle (money, health issues, negative people) or energetic obstacles (worry, fear of failure, negative self-talk). Whatever it is, name it now. It's as easy as tacking on a "but" to your desire statement from Step 1. My example: "I want to live in wild, creative expression in my personal and work lives, *but* I'm afraid that people won't get me or will think I'm too out there to take seriously."

Step 3: Write a series of "and" statements that bury your obstacle. Get bold with your "and" statements. Turn the positivity dial to 10 and write as many as you can. Create an avalanche of positivity. Make sure they're all written in the present tense. It's this easy; here's an example related to a real fear of mine and the affirmations I use to manage it: "I'm afraid that people won't get me or will think I'm too out there to take seriously, *and* . . .

- I have family and friends who believe in my big ideas."
- my quirkiness makes me unique; it attracts people I want to be around."
- I love to laugh; making people smile is one of my favorite things."

Use these three steps to create affirmations for every area of your life. Maybe you have wellness goals, but body image or health struggles are getting in the way. "I want to have a body I love and feel good in, but working out and eating healthy are big challenges for me." Counter that with "and" statements that create positive affirmations you can use again and again. "Working out and eating healthy are big challenges for me . . . *and* I'm dedicated, in this moment, to adopting simple ways of moving and eating that serve my goals" or "*and* every small effort I make makes me feel happier, stronger, and healthier right now."

Start with Integrity

Repeating positive affirmations helps keep your negative thoughts in check, but it's also important to keep your negative actions (or lack of actions) in check, too. I follow a pretty simple system for holding myself accountable. It's all about rules, consequences, and fessing up. My system keeps me feeling like I'm acting with integrity, and it's also getting me closer to my Grand Vision every day.

My thoughts, words, and actions are all part of a practice of integrity that gets me closer to that vision, closer to becoming the person who is living her dream life. What does "integrity" mean? It's simple. Integrity is saying you're going to do X and then doing X. Integrity is thinking, speaking, and acting in a way that supports your intentions and goals. It's being a wife, mother, sister, or friend who can be counted on to do the right thing, give the good advice, and offer the compassionate ear for their words or the soft shoulder for their tears. Integrity is keeping promises, especially the ones you make to yourself when no one else is looking.

All successes count—even the tiny ones, even the ones that look a lot like just surviving the day. But I slip up a lot, too. I say and do things that aren't in service to my Grand Vision. I yell at my kids. I neglect work deadlines. I make promises that I struggle to keep because I don't want to disappoint someone. I know integrity isn't a super-sexy word, but I promise it feels amazing to show up like the person you want to be, to say you're going to do X and actually following through instead of having to make excuses for having done Y.

How much time and energy have you wasted in feeling guilt, shame, regret, or embarrassment because you didn't show up the way you wanted to? Imagine how good it would feel to see someone you love and respect in the mirror each morning before starting your day. Or even better, imagine how good it would feel to make your dreams come true while your family watches and learns from your actions.

When my oldest child was still in diapers, I found a quote on the Internet and printed it on a small piece of paper. "My father did not teach me how to live. He lived and let me watch him do it." The quote hung on my refrigerator for almost two decades, and it's been at the heart of almost everything I do since the day I discovered it. My children are always watching, and I am always trying to do something worthy of their gaze, because I know my words matter so much less than my actions. It also reminds me that I must live for myself, too. My dedication to creating a life that is mine, a life that I love, also benefits my children. It teaches them how to create beautiful lives of their own.

Swap Excuses for Accountability

Elizabeth Gilbert, author of the bestsellers *Eat Pray Love* and *Big Magic*, famously said, "I've never seen any life transformation that didn't begin with the person in question finally getting sick of their own bullshit." I've been dreaming big dreams for a long time, much longer than I've spent making them come true. And I fell into a habit of making excuses for my fumbles and failures instead of owning up to and learning from them. Excuses never got me anywhere, so I needed to do something else. I was getting sick of my own bullshit—sick of feeling like I wasn't enough because I couldn't show up like I wanted. I needed to be held accountable for not sticking to my plans and promises in a way that allowed me to accept myself while also acknowledging where I might be falling short of my potential.

My process is simple. Let me walk you through each step.

Step 1: Review your Grand Vision. This is easy. Just look over what you imagined for yourself and wrote down on page 111. And just a side note here—I want you to feel inspired every time you read it. If imagining that vision of your future life stops feeling good in your body, feel free to revise it. My Grand Vision is always evolving, and you can expect yours to do the same.

Step 2: Pick one or two areas of your Grand Vision that you want to focus on every day, starting now. Whether it's your career, relationships, money, or health, choose whatever feels the most urgent or important to you to begin your work here. Great sex is on my list, so I'm committed to working on my romantic relationship with my husband on a daily basis. I've found that journaling is an easy way to connect with and support my vision, so I keep one that I'm *mostly* excellent at writing in.

You're going to assign a small action to these areas, so make sure you have the energetic space to work on them right now. I like to start with the most urgent. When I was struggling financially, I made working on my debt my highest priority. Seeing yourself make progress in the most difficult areas of your life will make working on other areas feel easy-peasy.

Step 3: Pick one or two things you need to *stop* doing because they get in the way of fulfilling your Grand Vision. Making a dream come true isn't only about adding things to do. You have enough on your schedule. Removing what isn't working is also essential. Think about it in terms of diet. You can add all the supplements you want, but if you're still eating fast food every day, are you ever really going to be healthy? You need to cut out the fast food!

Yelling used to be one of my worst habits, and it got in the way of my having strong relationships with my kids. I love watching them grow into adult people who I want to call my friends, and I want them to consider me a friend, too. And I can't tell you the last time that I yelled or screamed at a friend. Why would I think it's okay to do that to my own children? It hasn't been easy, but it's a behavior I've worked really hard (and am still working) to stop.

Step 4: Create some rules and a corresponding consequence for breaking each one. Rules are as easy as making a commitment to do or not to do something. I made a rule to never end a conversation (even a fight) with my husband without saying "I love you." And I can never go a day when we're together without kissing him and giving him a long embrace (I think I picked that one up from an *Oprah* episode 20 years ago). I make time to journal, even if it's just a bullet-point list of all the good and not-so-good things that happened that day. Yelling gets the zero-tolerance policy. No yelling, ever.

The consequences are not punishments. I mess up, and then I do better. I make the consequences playful but effective. If I fall short on hugs and kisses for my husband, I do something romantic for him the next day. If I don't journal, I commit to writing a motivational post for my Facebook group in which I share a personal struggle. And if I yell at anyone in my family—husband or children—no Netflix for 24 hours! (I know I said I don't want the consequences to feel like punishments, but I *really* want to stop yelling for good. A weird result of this is that I now deliver all my stern directives in a whisper-voice. It's totally creepy and freaks out the kids, but it works.)

Admitting your daily fumbles and correcting them is a practice of happy, successful people. Embrace the act of falling down and getting up again as the path to reaching all of your most important goals and the fulfillment of your daily success plan.

Step 5: Keep yourself in check with an accountability buddy. This is optional, but highly recommended. Every important undertaking takes a village, including raising up a better version of yourself. I have a small group of girlfriends who I consult with on a regular basis to do a "health check" for our respective goals and action steps. Knowing that I have to tell them when I mess up makes me mess up less. Holding my friends accountable to their goals makes me feel like I'm being of service to the people I care about.

Enlist a good friend, your partner, or even your online community as accountability buddies and check in with them often. It really works. I talk about my goals so much that I recently had one of my online community members rescue me from a croissant tray at an event: "You're giving up gluten, remember?" All right, I ate one, but I had been fully prepared to eat 10. Thanks, buddy!

Goals are yours to make, and success is something you get to define for yourself. Your Grand Vision and how you feel fulfilled every day are 100 percent up to you. I don't care if it's your life partner or a Pinterest mom with 2 million followers on Instagram trying to give you advice, what makes you happy is unique to your heart, your spirit, and your experience, and no one else gets the privilege of telling you what's right for you.

We all get to define success differently, and that definition might change from year to year, or even day to day. When my children were little, taking them on a day trip to the aquarium all by myself made me feel like the most accomplished woman on the planet. Now, I let my seven-year-old wear socks with Crocs to church because I'd rather spend the morning journaling than fighting over wardrobe choices. In both circumstances, I felt like a success. I felt like I was serving myself both in the moment and in the long term because I was supporting my happiness and the person I want to be. I get things done my way, on my terms, and however it feels good.

Invoking the words of the late, great Maya Angelou once more: "Success is liking yourself, liking what you do, and liking how you do it." When your actions match your intentions, your goals, and what makes your heart happy, you are doing success just as good as any CEO or rock star . . . or the mom who makes super-cute animal-shaped mini-sandwiches for her kid's lunches and includes a hand-drawn piece of art and a love note. She's doing her thing, and you get to do yours. You are removing the obstacles and turning pressure into vitality. That's how happiness works. That's how success looks and *feels*. And if you happen to be that Pinterest mom, please show me how to make Pokémon out of fruit slices.

CHAPTER 12

MANIFESTING YOUR DREAM RELATIONSHIPS

Seven days had passed, and I had hardly spoken to my husband. This was the way we worked through disagreements, a predictable (and unhealthy) pattern we had fallen into over the years. Something would happen, one of us would get upset, a confrontation would follow, and then, silence. We both work from home on most days, so it wasn't easy to navigate the silence without feeling suffocated by it. For me, someone who talks so much that I often do it out loud to myself, *not* talking about a problem feels like agony. I have to discuss the issue at hand. Otherwise, I just stew and simmer and boil over, exploding from the pressure.

I work hard not to be a yeller, and my husband has never been one, so loud back-and-forth fights rarely happen in our house. Screaming matches bring me right back to all the nights I spent awake in bed as a little girl, listening to my parents hurl insults and profanities at each other. They would wait until after my little sister's and my bedtime to fight, thinking we couldn't hear them. But, of course, we heard everything. And that verbal violence left an imprint on my soul, haunting me well into adulthood.

I made a promise to myself early in motherhood that my children would never suffer that. Needless to say, I broke that promise countless times in my first marriage, but eventually I learned to curb my instinct to lash out. Screaming triggered painful childhood memories, so avoiding it was more an act of self-protection than an evolved effort at better communication. I learned to stuff my feelings down because I didn't have a way to express them safely. Yelling hurt, so I held back. The silence was worse, though, because it felt like deprivation. I went from participating in emotional crimes to living in an emotional prison.

Choosing silence was also a way to avoid the frustration of never really fixing the problem. It was exhausting to keep having conversations that went nowhere because we were both unwilling to be honest and to fully accept each other's point of view.

I had to find a better way to resolve conflict, and I needed my husband on board to make that happen. I began to look at how my needing to be right and arguing until my husband submitted were really just milder expressions of verbal and emotional violence. Aggression, hurtful speech, and even retreating into silence were some of my parents' negative traits, and they were now showing up in me. It was up to me to break the cycle.

Winning an argument ultimately never felt good, anyway. There would be a brief rush of validation for being "right," and then I would be left with feelings of regret for how I had acted and with emptiness from knowing nothing had really gotten resolved. I felt like a bully every time, because I turned my husband into a loser. Why would I want to make anyone I love feel like a loser? Could I really have respect or romantic feelings for someone I perceived to be in that role?

I decided that for communication to feel loving and effective, there could be no losers. I believe manifestation takes place only when we are willing to take action, but also be flexible in our beliefs. If I wanted to manifest a better relationship with my husband, I needed to open myself up to learning new and better ways to show up in disagreement. I held the belief that honest and compassionate communication was possible. And I made a commitment to do whatever work was required to make that possibility a reality. The dictionary definition of "relationship" is the way in which two or more concepts, objects, or people are connected. Unresolved or unhealthy conflict creates separation, not connection. So, learning how to manifest my dream relationship—to create real, lasting, and fulfilling connection in my life—really just started out as a mission to learn how to fight better (or to not have to fight at all).

This is a good place for you to start, too. Learning how to connect in conflict is the perfect pathway to lasting love—of all kinds. When we can show up authentically and with loving compassion in our most challenging moments, it will feel even easier to create stronger, deeper bonds in the good times. You'll find that once you learn how to approach uncomfortable conversations with confidence, you'll start to manifest the relationships you've always wanted.

(Relationship) Fight Club

A post in one of the Facebook groups I belong to prompted the members to share our secrets for healthy, long-lasting relationships using just three words. Most of the responses were pretty standard lists like "communication, acceptance, commitment" or "understanding, trust, respect." There was another response that said, "walk my talk." I didn't have to think long before offering what I knew to be true for my relationship: "truth over comfort."

If I were to make a relationship version of *Fight Club*, the 1999 movie starring Edward Norton and Brad Pitt, the first rule would be "The truth is more important than your comfort." For me, staying comfortable in a disagreement meant staying attached to being right and reverting to my old, ineffective ways of expressing anger (yelling, manipulation, silence). It also meant not listening with an open mind. Instead, I would become defensive, deflecting instead of taking responsibility.

In our most recent debate, I got angry about how my husband was loading the dishwasher, convinced he wasn't even trying to do it right. When I accused him of purposely loading it like a drunk infant to drive me mad, he understandably felt that there was no way to do it "right." But I couldn't see that. All I could see was that my way was the right way, and if he would just do what I said, everything would be fine.

That's not a relationship. That's a hostage situation.

"You made me do it" was my favorite preschooler-inspired refrain, especially when it came to my parents. I blamed *every-thing* wrong in my life on Anne and Gary. And now I was doing the same thing to my husband. I needed new rules for negotiating conflict. Ironically, I discovered that most of the rules for the movie's Fight Club also work pretty well for Relationship Fight Club:

> **First and Second Rules:** *You do not talk about Fight Club.* I don't believe in keeping secrets. If there is something going on in your home that needs to be shared in order to resolve it, you share. But I also know there is nothing more devastating to a relationship than making your intimacies public (and trust me, as I'm writing a chapter about my marriage conflicts right now, I am very sensitive to this). But your mother-in-law, the Internet, and especially your children don't need to know about every dispute. There is a difference between sharing your truth and spreading your sh*t.

> ───────────

> **Third Rule:** *If someone taps out, the fight is over.* If your partner needs space, give it to them. Walk away, go for a run, pretend you're in the bathroom. Of course, make a promise to revisit the issue soon, and once you've calmed down, set a time to do so.

> ───────────

> **Fourth Rule:** *Only two guys to a fight.* Don't bring other people into your argument. Your sister doesn't need to tag in to tell your partner they're being a putz. And though it's good for children to see that conflicts can happen and be resolved, they don't need to be the audience to your Fight Club.

> ───────────

Fifth Rule: *One fight at a time.* Resist bringing up an old argument about the other person leaving the toilet seat up when you're trying to address your partner's obvious attempt to murder you by loading the dishwasher wrong.

Sixth Rule: *No shirts, no shoes.* No emotional weapons or stacking the deck against your partner. Fight clean.

Seventh Rule: *Fights will go on as long as they have to.* Commit to resolution. Or at least understanding.

Eighth Rule: *If this is your first night at Fight Club, you have to fight.* Try your best to engage when the opportunity presents itself. Don't fester for days (or weeks or years) in miserable passive-aggressive silence. And don't reject your partner's attempts at fixing an issue between you.

In dealing with conflict by yelling or stuffing away my emotions, I was clinging to my old, comfortable patterns, but that comfort was a sham. Instead, I was just creating a situation where I was constantly *un*comfortable. Never taking responsibility for my actions or handing the responsibility to someone else (to whom it didn't belong) made change impossible. And ghosting my husband when we're together practically 24-7 was a special kind of self-inflicted nonsense. I found myself wanting to share something funny I saw on Facebook and then forcing myself back into being pissed off at him, back into playing the silent-treatment game. I had to remind myself to stay mad! What's worse, sometimes I couldn't even remember why I was upset.

How many times have you avoided a difficult conversation only to find that your effort to avoid the drama just caused more drama? Or worked hard to summon anger even after you were pretty much over whatever it was that had gotten you mad in the first place? If you'd asked me, "Is this the hill you want to die on? How he loads the dishwasher—really?" I would have replied with a resounding "YES" every time. My readiness to make everything a battle, locked and loaded with prepared arguments, lists of offenses, and zero vulnerability, was my biggest obstacle in achieving ease in my relationship. I felt like I was "winning" a lot, but I was also exhausted from all the fighting.

I wish I could say that I have since learned how to stop that approach entirely, and that my relationship with my husband is now totally perfect, but that is not reality. Love is a work in progress, and every day is a chance to do it differently. Our relationships can either be the pressure that we need to grow and dream and succeed, or they can be the obstacles to our vitality.

I know that my first marriage wasn't the best source of inspiration. My life was really small during those years. But with Justin, I'm inspired by his love and I hope he's inspired by mine. The better we're able to work through the hard stuff (and there will always be hard stuff), the better we're able to be fueled by our love and respect for one another.

Stress needs to be able to move through you, and that means keeping energetic obstacles from blocking the flow. Because I was holding on to so much unreleased truth and holding back so much real emotion for the sake of looking strong and right, nothing moved with ease. Every external battle turned into an internal one. Outside pressure kept building (as it does), and I kept collecting and stacking rocks in my emotional stream. I piled them a mile high, and that kept me from processing anything—good or bad.

My husband and I had to find rules that would work for us in conflict. Because going in bare-knuckle wasn't actually authentic. It just meant we were both fighting from our worst places, and in the aftermath, neither of us got to be ourselves— the people we both were actually in love with. It was inauthentic to force myself to stay angry when I wanted to share something that made me smile. It was dishonest to stay silent when I really wanted to talk. And I was working totally out of alignment with my Grand Vision by turning every perceived offense into a battle. Although my stubbornness and negative behaviors are real aspects of my personality, I wasn't being authentic by wallowing in them. I wasn't telling the whole story if I was focused on only part of what I was feeling. My anger and disappointment were real, but what I wasn't sharing were my fears and my desires for a good outcome.

I spent seven days having one-sided conversations in my head, pouting around the house, and waiting for my husband to have some sort of epiphany that would lead him to ask me just the right questions and say just the right things. You know the script: "If you don't know why I'm mad, I'm not going to tell you." If I had just told him what was going on in my head, I could have avoided six days of unnecessary drama—or at least six days of the drama *about* the drama.

Cutting Off Your Arm to Spite Your Finger

Let's look at everyday relationship conflict like a paper cut on your finger. If your body is generally healthy, a paper cut is no big deal and will most likely heal on its own in a day or two. Likewise, if your relationship is generally healthy, something like a haphazardly loaded dishwasher isn't going to create any major drama. But let's say your immune system is compromised, or you handle something dirty without protecting the paper cut. You can expect it to get infected, and more attention and treatment will be required for healing. And what happens when you let the infection fester for too long without attention? Now, the infection is out of control, and you're amputating your arm— because of a paper cut.

That's dramatic, I know, but think about what happens when we ignore a minor conflict, when we let it grow, fester, and infect our relationships. Think about how any minor irritation (like not rinsing the dishes or forgetting to put the good wine glasses on the top rack) can feel like an assault instead of a small oversight. I know I'm not the only one to have a disagreement over household chores spin into a divorce-caliber fight. That's amputating an arm over a paper cut, but sadly, a lot of us do it.

When you have a disagreement with your partner, give it the attention it deserves. Treat it like a paper cut—care for it properly, clean it, apply the right medicine. Do it right away so it doesn't get infected. Don't play dirty when you're trying to heal. Speak honestly and openly about what's bothering you without bringing out a laundry list of offenses from all the time you've been together. Don't wait until your hurt feelings are taking up all the space in your head and ruining your day (or in my case, my whole week). Address the issue quickly to keep it from growing and festering. Don't cut off your partner because you let conflict grow into something too big to control. Remove the obstacles so you can allow the pressure of your love to become a vital force, and not a destructive one.

Letting the Real You Shine Through

The truth can feel uncomfortable, especially if you've had seemingly harmless discussions blow up into something much worse. Even hurt feelings—a completely normal reaction to hearing a difficult truth—can be enough to make you think twice before being direct.

As a species, human beings are pretty bad at telling and hearing the truth. We dance around the delivery of facts and feelings because being completely honest feels impolite. We want to be good and kind and compassionate, and that gets in the way of being honest. We want to avoid pain, but avoidance gets in the way of transformation. Being likable wins out over sharing what's real. The result of all this emotional evasion is even more undesirable than the initial pain we were trying to prevent. We move further and further away from authenticity and genuine relationships. We fail to experience resolution and personal growth.

"Find out who you are and do it on purpose."
— Dolly Parton

Honesty is at the root of every positive interaction. If you can't show up as your authentic self, who are you actually asking your partner (or friend, or child) to love? Presenting a watered-down or "nice" (or, alternatively, a hyperaggressive or defensive) version of yourself prevents the other person from ever really connecting with the real you. It blocks intimacy. Being truthful allows the real you to shine through. You make yourself available to be heard and to earn respect and genuine love from those around you.

Even little white lies can become unbearable to sustain over time. While still in the early months of dating my husband, I pretended to like outdoor camping. I wanted so badly for him to think I was interesting and adventurous that I spent hundreds of dollars on camping equipment I didn't want and couldn't afford and trekked into the wilderness for a "romantic" weekend together. Outside of spending time with the man I was falling in love with, every part of the trip was awful. I suffered countless bug bites and painful intestinal upset (I'm not down with pooping in the woods). The charade continued until I couldn't take it anymore (read: he put a ring on it). Now, the only camping we do together is in our backyard, and I usually escape to the indoors shortly after sunset.

This isn't anything compared to the big lies people tell and concessions they make for the sake of attracting love or achieving peace. The silliness of it all was that I was making myself miserable in order to find happiness. It made no sense. I'm lucky that "must adore wilderness camping" wasn't one of Justin's nonnegotiables. I'm grateful that there were many other parts of the real me that he loved. What I learned was that in every relationship, showing up as ourselves is the surest way to experience real and meaningful connection. Being truthful about everything, even when it puts us at risk for losing a relationship, is the only truly healthy approach.

But how can we be honest about the sticky parts of our relationships without damaging them? I know that if my partner took issue with something I was already sensitive about (like my appearance or a personality trait of mine that is hard to change),

I would be devastated. My 15-year-old told me recently that he was angry with me for putting him in the middle of an argument I was having with his father, my ex. It was painful to hear that I was hurting him with my actions, but I thanked him for being truthful and direct. Even though the truth can sometimes feel terrible to hear, it also offers us an enormous opportunity to show up better in our relationships.

How to Tell (and Hear) the Truth: The ICBD Method

Knowing how *not* to behave in our interactions is important. To increase vitality and flow, we must be willing to remove the obstacles that stand in their way. Fighting unfairly or not showing up authentically are unnecessary obstacles to manifesting your dream relationships. "Don't be a jerk" is good advice, but not sufficient for creating harmony between two people. It was easy to stop myself from showing up like an asshole, but I had to learn how to communicate better when I upgraded my relationship goals to include real growth and intimacy. I needed a guide to follow.

Every woman needs a girl gang. Mine is a group of super-bright, bighearted women (many of them working mothers, just like me) who get together in person and in group texts to support each other in work and in personal matters. We've shared ideas, personal tragedies and triumphs, lots of laughs, and a good amount of tears over the years. One member of our group, Alex Jamieson (co-creator and co-star of the Oscar-nominated documentary *Super Size Me* and a best-selling author), named our think-tank support sessions "mistressminds," an alternative to the very masculine-sounding "mastermind."

We were in one of our mistressmind sessions when Alex offered something she had been working on with her husband, Bob Gower. She presented a bullet-point version of their new project as I furiously transcribed her words onto the pages of my notebook. I knew it was something special before I even put it into practice. And soon, when I finally got to test it out for the first time with my husband, I knew it was a tool I couldn't live without.

Their ICBD method, which stands for Intentions, Concerns, Boundaries, and Dreams, has been a game-changer in my marriage—creating an intelligent framework for negotiations about everything from money to sex to who's doing what chore. And it's also changed the way I engage with my kids, my friends, and everyone else I love. In turn, it's changed the way they go out and engage with the world. ICBD is also in complete alignment with everything you've already learned on your journey through the pages of this book.

But for me, the real magic of this method is that it doesn't require two knowing participants to make it work. If just one person understands how to apply it, the interaction benefits all involved. Following the steps of the ICBD method taught me how to communicate all of my ideas better, and I hope it can do the same for you. Once you see how easy it can be to show up honestly and with clearly defined intentions, boundaries, and desires, manifesting a relationship that fully serves both parties will no longer be a dream. It will be your inevitable reality.

I'm offering you here a version of Alex and Bob's method integrated with my own practice. This is the same exercise I share with my coaching clients. To learn this technique straight from Alex and Bob and to dive even deeper into the work, visit their website, GettingToHellYes.com. It's a brilliant system that will change all of your relationships for the better.

Note that each step is far more effective when there's a back-and-forth, with each person taking a turn before moving on to the next step. Also, if you want to pull out this book to use in the middle of a conflict, it will not only be a great guide, it will also help take you and your partner out of the heat of the moment. Nothing feels more like a cold glass of water than going to the bookshelf and suggesting you follow a manifestation practice instead of engaging in a fight!

Here are the four easy steps that are going to rescue you from your next conflict.

Step 1: State your intentions. Why do you want to have this conversation? What's bringing you to the table? Think of this step as preparing the soil, creating fertile ground in which the conversation will take root and grow into something beautiful (or at least manifest into a better situation). This part doesn't require a lot of talking. Even when tackling something big and awkward like sex, it can be as simple as saying something like "Sexual gratification and intimacy are important to me, and I want us to have experiences that are satisfying for us both." Intentions are not demands. I used to show up to conversations like I was going into a political debate, prepared with mountains of evidence and quick comebacks for every objection. That was a recipe for disaster, not for peace and harmony. It made my husband put up his guard immediately and left no room for either party to be vulnerable.

Stating intentions without listing your expectations or demands allows your partner the space to prepare themselves without feeling backed into a corner. If you're the one who initiated the conversation, your partner might not have any intentions at the start. That's okay. You can take time for them to come up with one, or you can move on to the next step.

Step 2: Express your concerns. I used sex as the example because it's a sensitive topic that can be hard to explore without tension or nervousness. It might be one of the most-avoided conversation topics between couples (besides finances). I remember the first time I had to tell my husband that I didn't like something he did in bed. It was almost unbearably uncomfortable, and I wanted desperately to protect his feelings. Honesty without tact is cruelty, so compassion had to be a part of expressing my honest concerns. But if I wanted the issue resolved—if I wanted both of us to be winners—I had to talk about it. Listing my concerns at the beginning of the conversation helped to further create a safe space by letting him know that I cared about his feelings and wanted to avoid conflict.

This is the part where the seed we planted when we started the conversation is just beginning to crack open, and it's critical to be gentle while it's in this vulnerable stage. I said, "I'm

188

bringing this up because I want our sex life to be even better." That was a simple way to state my intention. Then I expressed my concern. "I know that it's hard to take feedback about something so intimate, and I'm afraid of hurting your feelings. Know that everything I say is being said with love and with the intention of making sex better for both of us." Now that your partner has heard your concerns, it's their turn to offer their own. Listen carefully, and don't interrupt. Give their words the attention you want them to give yours in return. This freedom to express whatever is weighing heavily on their heart will create an even greater feeling of safety and allow them to open up to you more easily in the future.

Step 3: Set clear boundaries. Boundaries can shift and change as the comfort level increases, but it's always important to honor where you and your partner are in the moment. Both parties need to be clear about what is and is not allowed during the conversation. I know I'm not ready to hear negative feedback about my body, so I make it known that comments about my appearance are off the table unless I specifically ask for them. My husband then has the chance to state his own boundaries that I promise to honor, no matter what.

What I found over time and with repeated success in using the ICBD method is that I felt safer and more willing to speak and hear truths that I would have run away from in the past. Also, as I mentioned earlier, taking ourselves out of emotion and into process gave us both the space we needed to communicate honestly. I learned that the rawer and more vulnerable we got in our conversations, the closer we felt toward each other. Setting boundaries is not only a method of self-protection, but also an act of self-care. Boundaries keep us safe and allow us to feel free. They're a way of both protecting and nourishing the relationship at once.

Step 4: Go wild with your dreams. It's impossible to let go of all expectations when starting an important conversation, so I'm not going to ask you to do that. One of the reasons I love

ICBD so much is because it lets us dream big and declare our desires out loud. I got to say, "Honey, I love you so much, and I want to have mind-blowing sex that leaves us both breathless every time. I want to feel free to tell you everything I want, and I want to give you exactly what you want." It's a final step that clears a path for so much more—for making big plans, expressing deeper desires, and being joyful in the process.

Not every conversation is about something as fun (or, maybe for you, nerve-racking) as sex. If it's with your kids, it might be about homework, chores, or a condom you found in your teenager's pants pocket (Lord, help me). But this approach works for every conversation, including the ones you have in your head. You can use also use the ICBD method on things that you need to work out on your own, including your relationship with yourself. Understanding what you want, the obstacles that are in your way, what you're willing and unwilling to tolerate in the course of making it happen, and having a dream (or Grand Vision) with which to align your actions makes every process feel purposeful. And it makes everyone involved in the interaction feel like a winner because no words were left unsaid and no voices were left unheard. In the end, the greatest joy comes when you get to watch the garden you planted bloom into something gorgeous.

Hide the Broccoli in the Mac 'n' Cheese

The truth will set you and everyone you love free. Even a toddler can spot a bullshitter when they see one, so why not just tell the truth? "I want you to go to bed. I know you don't want to, and I don't want you to be angry or sad. But no, you can't stay up past nine o'clock because that's my time to be with Daddy. I love you, and it's bedtime. You're going to have a good night's sleep, and we're all going to wake up happy in the morning." Intentions, concerns, boundaries, dreams. If it feels good, offer a reward for compliance—we *are* talking about toddlers, after all. (I will never judge a prudently executed bribe.) A temper tantrum might follow, but what's also happening is that your child is learning early on how to set boundaries for themselves. They're learning how to tell the truth, show concern and compassion, say yes and no, and create positive goals to work toward.

I can't promise you'll always get the perfect result from your older kids, either. Mine are champion eye-rollers and don't spare me from their moans and groans whenever I invite them to "have a talk" or participate in one of my latest personal-development experiments. That's fine. You know what to do— it's like hiding the broccoli in the mac 'n' cheese. Remember, this method works even if you're the only one who knows the steps. It's a secret weapon for doing good.

Manifesting *anything* is all about holding the vision for the dream outcome and keeping your actions aligned. Tweens and teenagers are masters of distraction, and the conversation steps you just learned will keep you on track and prevent you from going off the rails. Your kids don't need to know they're learning something that's good for them. As far as they're concerned, they're just having a peaceful, no-drama talk with Mom. All the lessons (the goodness that will nourish them for a lifetime) are hidden inside the experience.

Attract (the Good Parts of) What You Are

ICBD isn't just a framework for resolving conflict; it's also a powerful tool for attracting exactly the type of relationship you want. From the first pages of this book, I hope you've had the opportunity to hold a mirror up to your inner self, to discover what you desire most, and to find the tools and courage to express yourself freely. That's also the goal of ICBD: learning how to communicate effectively is learning how to express yourself honestly.

*"Only the truth of who you are,
if realized, will set you free."*
— Eckhart Tolle

And when you show up in full expression of who you truly are, letting the whole world know exactly what you want, you attract the same from others. You command respect.

In setting clear boundaries, we generate genuine love. We define what we are and aren't willing to tolerate in others, and we watch as the negative people, the energy vampires, and even the "haters" begin to leave our lives on their own. Because we're no longer giving them the energy they crave. They'll sense that their drama isn't welcome and take it somewhere else. We remove the obstacles to create vitality.

Just think of all the wonderful ways you can spend that extra time and emotional energy!

Now for the part I'm sure you've been waiting for: the happy ending to my seven-day standoff. Not long after our silent fight, I scheduled an interview with Alex and Bob in their Brooklyn apartment for my YouTube channel to help them promote the launch of *Getting to Hell Yes*. My husband tagged along as my cameraman for the shoot. Things were still tense between us, and I hardly spoke to him during the two-hour drive there and back. But he was inspired by what he heard in our interview and decided to dive into the method on his own.

He borrowed my copy of the book and started reading it that same night. The next day was a good one, and we even managed to work in a little not-quite-makeup-but-still-good sex. But when he sat down next to me the following morning and asked, "Can I have your attention for a little while to talk about something important?" I knew he was on board with ICBD.

He was initiating an important conversation!

He continued. "I want to talk about last night. I really like that thing you did, and I think we should do more of that. I'm concerned that you won't do it again if I bring it up, though. I know how you don't like talking about sex right after it happens, and I want to respect your boundaries. But yeah, I really want you to do that again. Your turn!" (I modified some of his actual words because you just don't need to know that much about me, but I do want you to know how easy having a tough conversation can be.)

Overnight, my husband had become an expert-level communicator—one who could express himself truthfully while respecting and listening to his partner. I was mortified, for sure, but I was also thrilled at what I recognized immediately as a new beginning in our relationship. Our standoff officially ended, and we started having better sex, too. How's that for a win-win?

Manifesting your dream relationships is about being true to who you are and knowing what you want. That can feel uncomfortable, and for some of us there's a big learning curve. But just because something might take a long time to work out or the subject matter goes deeper than we're ready for, it doesn't mean the path to healing has to be complicated. I promise you that the more you show up in truth, compassion, strength, and a real desire for a positive outcome, the more positive, healthy relationships will start to bloom in your life (and maybe even better sex, too!).

Meditation for Love and Connection

PREPARATION FOR YOUR MEDITATION

There's a saying that moves around in personal-development and spiritual-wellness circles that goes something like "You attract what you are." I've always had a little trouble with that statement because it is unfair and harmful to anyone who has suffered mistreatment. You're not a "bad" person if someone hurts you. But I do believe that when we are tapped into our truest state—one of confidence, connection, and self-love—we shine a light that demands to be seen and admired. Our energy is like a lighthouse that calls love home from all directions. Think about the most confident woman you know. Doesn't it feel good just to *be* in her presence?

POSITION / BREATH / GAZE

This meditation is an invitation for love and connection, so I recommend placing one or both of your hands over the center of your chest (your heart space) during your practice. Feel your chest rise and fall under your hand as you move through your breath cycles. Can you feel your heartbeat? Let that be a reminder of the powerful life force moving within you.

WORDS FOR YOUR PRACTICE

Read your words aloud in a whisper and with your hand placed over your heart space. See if you can match the cadence of your speech with the rhythm of your heartbeat, connecting physical expression with the physical feeling in your body. Check in with yourself as you read, and notice any emotional response that shows up.

Time and circumstances have added layers of fear and doubt and insecurity upon my heart, but there is a light inside me that cannot be dimmed.

As I peel back the layers, one by one, in the spirit of self-discovery, my light shines even brighter for the whole world to see. My gorgeous, shiny spirit is a lighthouse that guides love home to me.

As I let go of the opinions of others, of self-judgment, and of negative stories, I allow for a clear path to connect to the true and radiant nature of who I am. I connect to my inner brilliance easily and with joy. I rewrite my narrative from a place of pure love, held by the warmth of my own bright light.

YOUR MANTRA

Continue to hold your hand over your heart space. Feel your chest expand as it fills with your breath and fall as you exhale. Notice your heartbeat. How has it changed since you began your meditation? Notice your breath. Imagine every inhale as a way of welcoming loving energy to move through your body, and every exhale as sending your love back out into the Universe. Repeat your mantra either silently or out loud on the exhale of every breath, pausing each time at the bottom.

I am a lighthouse calling love home. I attract love and support from every direction.

BLOOM, BABY, BLOOM!

CHAPTER 13

IT'S TIME TO CELEBRATE

Every Sunday at my church, we pick an affirmation card from a bowl. One particular Sunday, I prayed that my card would inspire me for the busy and demanding week ahead. It was going to be one of those weeks that would require powering through a lot, and I was okay with that. Some weeks are just plain tougher than others, and I wanted a little nudge from the Universe to push me forward.

As I approached the bowl, I repeated a silent prayer to myself. I asked for my hand to be guided to pick just the right card, and I reached into the bowl knowing that this was going to be the message that would sustain my soul for the next seven days. Perhaps I was a little overconfident in my powers of divination, because my affirmation couldn't have been less inspirational.

I'm usually good at finding a lesson in just about anything, but my efforts to pull any meaning out of my card fell flat. It read: "Money is simply energy and an exchange of services. How much I have depends on what I believe I deserve." First of all, I'm not going to get into how problematic that statement is in general, but I will say that it was decidedly unhelpful (and unrelated) when it came to easing my worries that week. I returned to my seat feeling deflated.

"I don't need your ultra-spiritual financial advice right now, Karen!" I wanted to yell. (I sometimes call the Universe/God

"Karen" when I'm annoyed or frustrated. It makes me feel like Ray Liotta's character in *Goodfellas* when he melts down after learning his wife dumped all the drugs down the toilet: "Why!? Why did you do that, Karen?" Whyyyyy!?)

Luckily (or *divinely*), things turned around after the service. I usually try to attend the fellowship hour, when the congregants sit down together for refreshments and snacks, and that day I *really* needed some fellowship. I was standing in the food line when I remarked that I would be skipping the cake and filling my plate with fruit and salad instead. Miss Jean, one of our esteemed church elders exclaimed, "What would you do *that* for? You look great!"

I laughed and scooped some more salad onto my paper plate. She and I made our way to one of the big tables in the back of the community space and continued the conversation about how good all the food looked and how I wouldn't be having most of it. Miss Jean asked why, and I told her I'd been dealing with some health issues that I was trying to work through without medication. I went on to say how tired I'd been and how I couldn't wait for the kids to go back to school so I could focus on resting and getting back to a manageable work routine.

Miss Jean laughed. "I had seven kids and a job. And no husband! He left me when my oldest was 12. I hated exercise, I ate meat, and I smoked cigarettes. I smoked other stuff, too!" I howled with shock and delight as she went on.

"I'm 84 years old. My oldest is 67. I have twenty-some grandkids and the same number of great-grandkids. I can't remember all their names or how many there are exactly. But that's okay. Grandkids won't pay you no mind."

Tears filled the corners of my eyes and I could feel my mouth—my whole face—smiling big. I laughed until I cried. Here was this amazing woman, who I would never think of judging, telling me just how imperfect her own parenting was. And the thing was, I had seen the results of her work. Her children and grandchildren were amazing. They adored her. She was clearly still the light of their lives.

And she hadn't followed any of the rules that I kept trying to apply to myself.

I mean, I wasn't going to run out and grab a pack of smokes, but I realized that Miss Jean had done the best she could do in the conditions she was given, as a single mother raising seven kids on her own. In my own way, I was just trying to do the same. I could only surrender to the conditions. Fighting them had only left me more stressed and more judgmental of my every move.

Two other women chimed in with stories about their adult sons and how they struggled with them growing up. We laughed some more and shared words of wisdom and comfort between us. Then Miss Jean shared that she was worried about one of her grandsons, and about the choices *he* was making, so I offered her my own advice: no matter what our children (or grandchildren) are going through, we can still hold a vision of them having a wonderful future despite what's happening now. No matter where they're at in life, a beautiful future is possible.

Miss Jean patted my hand and said, "I'm going to remember that." (You see, we all have wisdom to share with each other, across generations and from every stage of experience.) I told Miss Jean I would write about her in this book because I felt so blessed by our conversation. And as I sat there, fully present and soaking up all the goodness of that table of women, I knew that my earlier prayer was being answered. Forget the affirmation card; Miss Jean was my gift from the Universe, my inspiration that I could handle anything that lay ahead.

I didn't decide to start smoking cigarettes or eating junk food, but I did extend myself some grace with one of the most healing and simplest affirmations I know. I use this one a lot and offer it to moms and clients who are in the middle of their own intense transitions: *This is normal. Everything is going to be okay. I promise.*

The thing about motherhood is that you never know how anything is going to turn out, but you can hold faith that it will all be okay. I've done many good things, lots of bad things, some good things that I found out later were bad, and things that I said I would never do but that wound up being the best thing for the situation. Each one of my kids is turning out so different from the others (talk about nature versus nurture), and I hold space for each of them to have a beautiful future, too.

I hope to live as long as Miss Jean (she assured me I *will* survive motherhood, even though on a lot of days, that feels doubtful). And I am holding the vision of seeing my grandchildren grow up to have babies of their own. But I won't worry too much about how they'll turn out. They won't pay me no mind, anyway. And I hold faith that they'll be okay.

But no matter what happens along the way and every day, I'm going to keep giving myself grace and crying happy tears over the beautiful moments—like that one with Miss Jean. Thank you, Universe, for answering my prayer.

Behold the Blooms as Proof of Your Potential

Miss Jean didn't tell me her life was perfect. Quite the contrary, she had lived a hard life. And yet there she was, smiling and laughing and offering me comfort—"You're gonna be all right." And I was obliged to believe her. Miss Jean's presence commanded my faith in her message.

This is what blooming looks like—surviving the moments, finding the lessons, knowing that you did your best, and calling it all success. Planting, nourishing, weeding, celebrating the harvest, turning over the soil, and starting over, again and again and again.

I want you to feel success in your own life, just like Miss Jean, and to enjoy the fruits of your labor without worry or hesitation. I want you to be able to love up all over yourself because you do so much! You deserve it! And besides, it's good for everyone around you to witness the love you have for yourself. Our children learn from watching, and because I watched my mother battle her own self-doubt, I recognize the greatest gift I can give my kids is to celebrate myself.

Celebrating ourselves teaches our children to celebrate their own accomplishments, and through self-love we inspire them to love themselves. As nurturers we also show up as joyful leaders with powerful influence, acknowledging our personal achievements and inspiring independence and self-determination in our children. We are then able to spread our joy to our families and communities—seeds of joy that will thrive, bloom, and manifest into even more love in this world.

Release by Fire

Before we get to our final exercise (I can't believe we're already there!), I have one more quick ritual for you. I want you to make a list of negative feelings or beliefs you wish to leave behind for good. You're going to write them down as declarations of release, as in "I release feeling unworthy of celebration," or "I release my guilt over pursuing my dream job."

Try to write at least five statements about whatever's weighing you down right now. After you have your complete list, build yourself a fire. I like to use my fireplace, a pot on the stove, or an outdoor firepit, but you can even use an imaginary fire inside a box or trash can. Now, read each statement out loud before tossing the list into the fire. Imagine those negative beliefs disintegrating as your list is consumed and destroyed by the flames. Close your eyes, take a deep, letting-go breath, and release yourself from the bonds of those beliefs, once and for all. And, of course, remember to practice safety first and have a fire extinguisher nearby! *Said in my most stern Mom voice.*

What Other People Think of You Is None of Your Business

It can be so hard, almost impossible, to move through this world unbothered by the gazes and opinions of other people. Just feeling like we're enough takes effort. The work you've done during the course of this book—even if you've only run through the activities in your head—has hopefully given you a greater sense of confidence that allows you to embrace motherhood in your own way. Happiness, when defined by other people's standards or opinions, is fragile. It's critical that we believe in success in our own right, and that our standards are the only ones that matter. But how do we get to that place of belief? Where can we find that evidence to make our beliefs stand up to the criticism of others (and more important, our own self-criticism)?

Intellectually, I understand that my self-worth can't be tied to other people's opinions of me. I think you get that, too, at least by now. "What other people think of me is none of my business" is one of my favorite woman-in-total-control-of-herself mantras that I repeat often to affirm my independence and my right to feel good about myself. But it fails me when I try to replace the words "other people" with "my children." My children are pieces of my heart that exist outside of my own body. I want little more than for them to feel fully loved by me and to feel their love in return. While I give myself grace in the understanding that my children's opinions of me will ebb and flow with time, and that those feelings have little to nothing to do with my value as a woman or a mother, at least for now my happiness and sense of accomplishment are tightly tied to the health of my relationship with each child. I know this and have surrendered to that truth.

But that ebb and flow of feelings of love, happiness, and success makes it hard to always sit in a place of celebration and declare, "Yes, I did it! I did motherhood well." Because when will that ever really feel true? When can we finally say our job of mothering is done and gather the evidence that will allow us to claim our reward? My oldest is a bright, beautiful, and independent college junior, and I know I have many years of mothering her ahead of me—years that I look forward to with gleeful enthusiasm (and I mean that). I welcome every laundry pile carted home on semester breaks and each phone call telling me she's "fine," but "wouldn't mind a visit." In that moment, a last-minute five-hour drive to meet her at school feels like the greatest privilege (and gift) I can receive.

So, where do I get the final grade that stamps my imaginary mothering report card with a big, bold JOB WELL DONE, REBEKAH?

Nowhere. That proof doesn't exist. My children will be my babies until the day I leave this earth. But just like you planted the seeds for your dream life by writing your Grand Vision statement, there's a way to imagine a beautiful future where you have accomplished everything you wanted to, where your children deliver the proof of your success. There's a way to remind ourselves of the good job we have already done—and why that is indeed worthy of celebration. Grab your journal (or whatever you're using to record your work for this book) and a box of tissues. Let's celebrate together.

Dear You, Love Me

I keep pictures of my parents on my refrigerator and on my desk, places I visit every day, and I talk to them often. That talk usually takes the form of a silent prayer or a smile. If one of the kids is around, I'll tell a happy story about Mom-Mom or Grandpop that makes us both smile or elicits a question about what they were like when I was little.

This past Father's Day, five years after my dad's death, I wrote him a note—a love letter.

> Hey Dad,
>
> I think of you often. How excited you'd be about all the things I have going on right now. How you would cry whenever you looked at the picture that sat on your desk of Sunny in the Phillies baseball outfit. How much you'd love Annie.
>
> I think about your childlike wonder. How afraid you were of dying even though your life was the hardest of anyone I've ever known. How happy you were that I found someone to love and made a family with him. How much you loved God. How worried you would get whenever I traveled because "the world is dangerous" (you believed everything you saw on TV). The art we would make. The adventures we would take. Collecting cans. Cleaning up discarded curbside bicycles. Transforming trash into treasure. You were an alchemist—a magic man.

Your silly grin that would hide the teeth you didn't have the money to fix. Your white T-shirts and Wrangler jeans. The smell of sawdust and tar on everything you touched. How you sat in your pickup and waited for my friends and me every week outside the skating rink. How much you loved cigarettes, sugar, and Downtown Julie Brown.

I miss you so much. You were the first person to truly choose me . . . and the person who kept choosing me my whole life, every day, unconditionally. I'm so lucky to have experienced that. Too few humans do.

Love, Bekah

I realized as I was writing that then that these were things I had never said before. Tears filled my eyes as I imagined how happy it would have made my father to hear any of that from me when he was still alive. He doubted himself in so many areas of his life. Knowing his daughter held him in high esteem would have meant the world to him.

A Love Letter from Your Child(ren)

"I gave her my heart, she gave me a turd."
— Christine DiPilla

The above quote came from a Facebook post where my friend, Christine DiPilla, a Reiki master and intuitive bodyworker, wrote about a typical day with her toddler. I remember the story being about her youngest daughter, Penelope, handing her a present that turned out to be Penelope's poop. That pretty much sums up 90 percent of the motherhood experience. We give our children our whole hearts, and we're lucky when we get a pile of poop in return.

I know my children love me, but I might wait a lifetime to hear the exact words that would allow me to feel like I did a good job. I might never hear them at all—as with my dad and me. So, I decided that I would have to write my own love letter from my children to myself, and I'm inviting you to do the same.

It wasn't until after I lost both my parents that I really saw their humanity and appreciated all the aspects of who they were. That's just one of the hazards of the parent-child relationship. They were my parents, and parents aren't actual human beings—are they? Only later can we understand the physical fatigue, the endless worry, and the immeasurable heartache that goes into raising children. We can't expect children to "get it" or appreciate parenthood fully—well, maybe after they have their own kids. And that still doesn't mean they're going to connect with us. I know it was hard for me even after having children of my own to empathize with my mother's journey into motherhood. Sadly, it wasn't until after her death that I realized she was just doing the best she could with what she had. How I wish I had only said those words sooner, and to her.

You're going to put all of that into your love note. This is *different*, I know, but I promise it will feel good. I want you to imagine yourself as your grown child (or one of your grown children) reflecting on their childhood and expressing how loved they felt, how grateful they are, and how much they love you for all you've done for them. Let this love letter live in your heart as a prediction as well as a celebration. I'll get you started by offering a short version of one I wrote for myself, authored by one of my adult daughters and sent from a time in the not-so-distant future.

Dear Mom,
I just finished putting the little ones to bed, and it's the first quiet moment I've had to myself in a week. I forgot to thank you for coming by the other day and taking care of the kids while I got that work project done. Everything feels so overwhelming these days, and I'm barely holding it together. I want you to know that I really appreciate your help. It feels good to be able to count on you to be there when I need you.

I know you worked hard at taking care of our family—you reminded us of that a lot—but you still made it look so easy. I never realized just how much goes into taking care of a house and a family. And you did it all while going after your big dreams! I remember the summer you wrote your book about being a mom—how you were crying every other day, saying you wanted to quit. You would haul your laptop to soccer games and write before dawn and after we went to bed. And I remember how you would celebrate after you finished each chapter by dancing around the house and ordering Chinese food. Now, I finally understand how hard it must have been to keep that dream alive and why it felt like such a huge accomplishment when you finished.

By the way, thank you for that. Thank you for showing me that there's more to life—to being a woman—than just taking care of other people. Thank you for showing me how to make time for my partner and my own big dreams. I know we kids weren't always easy to manage with everything we had going on, and I know I've said some pretty harsh stuff to you over the years, but I get it now. I sometimes feel lost in motherhood, but your example reminds me to never stop searching for myself and to always celebrate what I discover.

I guess I just want you to know that I appreciate who you are. This mom thing is super hard, but I know I'll be good at it because you showed me how. You gave us a lot, and that makes it easy for me to give a lot to my kids. And thanks again for rescuing me from my out-of-control day last week—my project was a huge success! I love you, Mom.

Now, it's time to write your own love letter. You might have noticed that a few of the things I mentioned were things I've felt guilt over. I didn't want to be the mom on the sidelines of a soccer game with her face buried in a laptop, but that was the only way to get this book done on time. So this letter doesn't just serve as wishful thinking, it's also a powerful tool for forgiveness. It's a way to acknowledge the love that might go unnoticed by your kids but that you know is at the core of everything you do.

The practice of writing your love letter can be incredibly healing, but I get that it might not feel quite like a celebration. Honestly, there aren't a ton of conventional *woo-hoo!* moments in motherhood, unless you count the thrill of that first five minutes of having a perfectly clean house right before company arrives. (Seriously, how sweet are those fleeting moments when it looks like nobody lives in your house?)

Managing the motherload (for me, at least) has been roughly 50 percent wondering if I'm doing it right, 45 percent pretending like I'm doing it right, and 5 percent feeling like I might actually be doing it right. That 5 percent is where I celebrate (and rest, and heal, and grow). I know it doesn't sound like much, but that 5 percent is actually huge. I think you know how a baby's uncontrolled giggles can be the cure for just about anything bad. Let those giggles be a mini-celebration at the end of a really hard day. After all, how many things have ever made you feel better than that?

I'm dealing with a lot in my own life right now, and I don't know if there will ever be a time when that will be different. Because . . . it's motherhood! Pressure is relentless, but so is my practice to keep it flowing through me. And in those moments when I'm moving closer to my Grand Vision and further from the obstacles that hold me back and block my flow, I'm gonna celebrate, sister. It's in those moments of pure flow when I realize that all the work is worth it.

Because for all the pressure I feel, I have a lot to celebrate, too. My youngest daughter's birthday is this weekend, so I held my breath and texted my oldest son an invitation to her party. He said yes! We've actually been communicating about a few other things, but I'm treading lightly. The old me would put pressure on the situation to make it better, and fast. Now I understand that force has little to do with love. I've learned to surrender to the slow, unfolding process of nurture meeting nature. I am going to keep showing up with patience and nonjudgment, even as I allow him to grow at his own pace and on his own terms. And I am going to accept that I won't always practice that perfectly. All I can do is carefully remove the weeds that try to crowd out the new growth, and then let sunlight, rain, and time do their jobs. And when a new bud (an answered text or invitation, a hug, or an "I love you") appears, I will celebrate it with my whole heart. That's how healthy gardens grow and bloom.

Motherhood is a tough gig, but one filled with a kind of joy incomparable to any other happiness in this lifetime. My practice is to surrender judgment and allow all those tiny moments to feel big in my heart. I want you to do the same for your tiny moments. You deserve to celebrate them all. Know that I'm celebrating with you.

Whether you're just starting out on your motherhood journey or you've been at it for a while, it will never stop teaching you, and you will never stop defining it. You are in it, sister! And that means that motherhood is yours to create, reinvent, and celebrate again and again, every day of your life. I thought it would be perfect to end the book with a meditation for new beginnings and for calling in all the brilliant, beautiful, and bountiful blessings that are waiting for you to harvest. This is your time to begin again, with new tools, greater wisdom, and a gorgeous new outlook for today and all the days ahead.

P.S. Congratulations for making it to the end of a whole book (written for adults)! You're a rock star, Mama.

Meditation for New Beginnings and Blessings

PREPARATION FOR YOUR MEDITATION

This is your final meditation, but it's meant to mark a new beginning for you. You have all the tools to nurture and bring to full bloom a version of love, success, and fulfillment that is completely and uniquely yours. I want this meditation to feel like a celebration of what you've already accomplished and a declaration of all the good you have left to give and receive. You are a mother, the center of creation and a vessel for divine wisdom. Own it!

POSITION / BREATH / GAZE

I'd love for you to practice this meditation outdoors or in front of an open window where you can feel the sun and experience at least some outside elements. Immerse yourself in all of the splendor of Mother Nature during your practice. Use whatever breathing technique feels good for you. Notice how it feels to inhale the fresh air. Send your exhale out into the world and imagine it mingling with the breaths of the flowers and the trees. Close your eyes to imagine an even more idyllic scene, or open them to behold the beauty that's in front of you.

WORDS FOR YOUR PRACTICE

I wrote these words in tribute to the origins of the practice I've shared with you throughout this book. It's a prayer for guidance, support, Divine Discernment, wisdom, and celebration. Read it knowing that it was written with love.

Gentle Universe, allow me to become aware of what's been planted, and which seeds have cracked open for me. Grace me with the wisdom to nurture for now only what I can support emotionally, physically, and spiritually. Make clear the action steps that will bring what's sprouted to full bloom. Compel me to enjoy the fruits of my labor. Let me find comfort in surrendering to a process that nurtures my happiness. And so it is.

YOUR MANTRA

If you remember only one mantra from this book, I hope this is it. Take a big, deep, energizing inhale, and let it all go. Inhale and exhale once more. Smile. Now, read the mantra and commit it to memory before you close your eyes. Repeat it on every breath cycle of your meditation. But don't let it stop there. For the rest of your day and all the days that follow, remind yourself of the work you did here by repeating the mantra to yourself. This one is yours—believe in its power as a reflection of your own.

I am a mother, a creator, and creation itself.
I am the Universe and boundless love.

ACKNOWLEDGMENTS

"Write about motherhood in 60,000 words." I took on that task with enthusiasm and also a little worry. I used to joke that any book I wrote about parenting wouldn't be longer than a single page. "Step 1: Toss all the parenting books (and unsolicited advice). You are already wise. Step 2: Do the best you can today. I mean, seriously, what more can you do than that? Step 3: Do your best tomorrow. And so on. Bonus Step: Accept that in many ways both good and annoying, you *will* become your mother, and everything will be just fine." I would fill the rest of the page with a picture of myself nursing a baby with bits of leftover grilled-cheese sandwich in my hair and a laptop resting on my thighs. Because, after all, that or some variation of it is my real life most of the time (and I love it).

How could I possibly fill a book with advice I never wanted to give, that I felt unqualified to offer? I wanted to say no and move on to the next best opportunity. Loving words of encouragement from family, friends, and colleagues (and lots of time in meditation) pushed me toward a big yes in accepting the challenge. Like I said in the introduction, even though it's been a bumpy road (one I'm still traveling, by the way), I'm truckin' along just fine. I'm still here, breathing through public temper tantrums, laughing with my husband when we wake up next to each other in a kid-pee-soaked bed, and succeeding at some semblance of competency in pursuing my big dreams. I'm going for it every day, and come hell or high water (we've dealt with a lot of clogged toilets and bathroom floods during the potty-training years), I'm going to come out of this raising-small-humans thing alive. Better than that—I'm going to do it with big smiles, ugly cries, and unapologetic celebrations of every tiny win. Not to mention tons of grace and forgiveness.

I said yes to writing this book because I know that all my success in motherhood is a result of the good stuff I have learned along the way (from a lot of wise women and men, and even a few books!). And I knew that was a message worth sharing. So, the revised version of that single-page book is what you just read. And now it's time to give some thanks.

When I was just a baby, a neighbor "adopted" me. She was 25 years old and child-free. Over the years, especially during my parents' rocky separation, she fed my little sister and me, let us play at her house, bandaged our skinned knees, gave us holidays like Christmas and Easter, and even took us on summer vacations to the Jersey shore. I'm so grateful for my "Aunt" Kathy, who stepped in and filled in the gaps in my family life. Families can be successful in many forms, but every family needs a village. That village can be your neighborhood or an online community. It can be extended family or trusted friends. But we all need help. I'm here because of a village. Thank you, Aunt Kathy.

Today, so many gorgeous souls populate my village, some of whom support me in my personal growth while others offer professional guidance that helps me reach more people with my work.

Thank you to my literary agent, Wendy Sherman, for believing in my voice and guiding me with wisdom and compassion. To my editors, Corinne Bowen and Kristen McGuiness, you pulled the stories out of me and made a sometimes-daunting process feel like fun. I couldn't have done this without you. And to my Hay House family, especially Mary Norris, thank you for helping me share these lessons with the world.

My online community inspires me every day. Thank you to everyone who has ever read one of my blogs, meditated with me on YouTube, bought my first book, joined my Facebook group, or shared your stories with me. I am blessed to be able to walk the path of healing and self-discovery with you.

Thank you to my mentors, Lauren Handel Zander and Catrice Jackson, and to all my friends and colleagues whose work I shared on these pages, most notably Michael Perrine,

Elizabeth DiAlto, Grace Smith, Anna Gannon, John Halcyon Styn, Danny-J, Amy Kate LeRoy, Erin Stutland, Jennifer Pastiloff, Alexandra Jamieson, Bob Gower, and Christine DiPilla.

For being my purpose, my reason, and my greatest teachers, thank you to Winona, Calvin, Jack, Sunny, Annabel, and Justin. Because of you, I am.

ABOUT THE AUTHOR

Rebekah "Bex" Borucki, founder of BEXLIFE® and the BLISSED IN® wellness movement, is a mother of five, TV host, meditation guide, author, speaker, and birth doula. She shares glimpses of her family life and her work as a meditation guide and life-transformation and resilience coach with her vibrant and engaged online community on social media through multimedia content daily. Bex also travels extensively, sharing her love for yoga, wellness, and meditation at workshops, retreats, and public events. Visit her at BexLife.com.

Hay House Titles of Related Interest

YOU CAN HEAL YOUR LIFE, the movie,
starring Louise Hay & Friends
(available as a 1-DVD program, an expanded 2-DVD set,
and an online streaming video)
Learn more at www.hayhouse.com/louise-movie

THE SHIFT, the movie, starring Dr. Wayne W. Dyer
(available as a 1-DVD program, an expanded 2-DVD set,
and an online streaming video)
Learn more at www.hayhouse.com/the-shift-movie

*DO LESS: A Revolutionary Approach to Time and Energy
Management for Busy Moms,* by Kate Northrup

*THE RISE: An Unforgettable Journey of Self-Love, Forgiveness,
and Transformation,* by Danette May

THE UNIVERSE HAS YOUR BACK: Transform Fear to Faith,
by Gabrielle Bernstein

*LET YOUR FEARS MAKE YOU FIERCE: How to Turn Common
Obstacles into Seeds for Growth,* by Koya Webb

All of the above are available at your local bookstore,
or may be ordered by contacting Hay House (see next page).

We hope you enjoyed this Hay House book. If you'd like to receive our online catalog featuring additional information on Hay House books and products, or if you'd like to find out more about the Hay Foundation, please contact:

Hay House, Inc., P.O. Box 5100, Carlsbad, CA 92018-5100
(760) 431-7695 or (800) 654-5126
(760) 431-6948 (fax) or (800) 650-5115 (fax)
www.hayhouse.com® • www.hayfoundation.org

———

Published in Australia by:
Hay House Australia Pty. Ltd., 18/36 Ralph St., Alexandria NSW 2015
Phone: 612-9669-4299 • *Fax:* 612-9669-4144 • www.hayhouse.com.au

Published in the United Kingdom by:
Hay House UK, Ltd., Astley House, 33 Notting Hill Gate, London W11 3JQ
Phone: 44-20-3675-2450 • *Fax:* 44-20-3675-2451 • www.hayhouse.co.uk

Published in India by: Hay House Publishers India,
Muskaan Complex, Plot No. 3, B-2, Vasant Kunj, New Delhi 110 070
Phone: 91-11-4176-1620 • *Fax:* 91-11-4176-1630 • www.hayhouse.co.in

———

Access New Knowledge.
Anytime. Anywhere.

Learn and evolve at your own pace
with the world's leading experts.

www.hayhouseU.com